THE ENCHAFÈD FLOOD

These lectures were delivered at
the University of Virginia under
the Page-Barbour Foundation on
March 22, 23, 24, 1949.

THE ENCHAFÈD FLOOD

or
The Romantic Iconography
of the Sea

W. H. AUDEN

UNIVERSITY PRESS OF VIRGINIA

CHARLOTTESVILLE

ISBN 0–8139–0827–2 (cloth)

ISBN 0–8139–0828–0 (paper)

Manufactured in the United States of America

ACKNOWLEDGMENT

I WISH TO EXPRESS MY THANKS to the University of Virginia and the trustees of the Page-Barbour Lecture Foundation under whose auspices the contents of this book were given in lecture form during March, 1949.

Thanks are also due to the following for the use of their translations in quotation: Kathleen Freeman (*Pre-Socratic Philosophers*), Margaret Williams (*The Wanderer and the Sea-Farer*), Alexander Dru and Walter Lowrie (Kierkegaard), Christopher Isherwood (Baudelaire's *Journals*), Helen Zimmern (Nietzsche), Helen Rootham, Norman Cameron and Delmore Schwartz (Rimbaud), Edwin Muir (Kafka).

W. H. A.

CONTENTS

ONE

The Sea and the Desert

∿∿∿∿∿∿∿

Adama: O Adam, when blew God that bitter breath
        On Earth's Plain; blew He likewise on sea-deep?

Adam: I wiss not. Like to cragged desolate waste,
        We lately passed, is sea-steep's haggart face.

C. M. DOUGHTY, *Adam Cast Forth*

Revolutionary changes in sensibility or style are rare. The most famous is, perhaps, the conception of '*amor*' which appeared in Europe in the twelfth century. The disappearance, during the sixteenth, of allegory as a common literary genre is another. The complex of attitudes and styles which emerges towards the end of the eighteenth century and is called, more conveniently than accurately, Romanticism is a third.

These chapters are an attempt to understand the nature of Romanticism through an examination of its treatment of a single theme, the sea.

*

Near the beginning of the fifth book of *The Prelude*, Wordsworth describes in some detail a dream. It is, perhaps, an indication that, to him, this dream was of particular importance, that the 1805 and the 1850 versions differ. In the first it is assigned to a friend, in the second to Wordsworth himself. This is the 1805 text.

2

. . . once upon a summer's noon,
While he was sitting in a rocky cave
By the sea-side, perusing, as it chanced,
The famous History of the Errant Knight
Recorded by Cervantes, these same thoughts
Came to him; and to height unusual rose
While listlessly he sate, and having closed
The Book, had turned his eyes towards the Sea.
On Poetry and geometric Truth,
The knowledge that endures, upon these two,
And their high privilege of lasting life,
Exempt from all internal injury,
He mused: upon these chiefly: and at length,
His senses yielding to the sultry air,
Sleep seiz'd him, and he pass'd into a dream.
He saw before him an Arabian Waste,
A Desart; and he fancied that himself
Was sitting there in the wide wilderness,
Alone, upon the sands. Distress of mind
Was growing in him, when, behold! at once
To his great joy a Man was at his side,
Upon a dromedary, mounted high.
He seem'd an Arab of the Bedouin Tribes,
A lance he bore, and underneath one arm
A Stone; and, in the opposite hand, a Shell
Of a surpassing brightness. Much rejoic'd
The dreaming Man that he should have a Guide
To lead him through the Desert; and he thought,
While questioning himself what this strange freight
Which the Newcomer carried through the Waste
Could mean, the Arab told him that the Stone,
To give it in the language of the Dream,

Was Euclid's Elements; 'and this,' said he,
'This other,' pointing to the Shell, 'this Book
Is something of more worth.' And, at the word,
The Stranger, said my Friend continuing,
Stretch'd forth the Shell towards me, with command
That I should hold it to my ear; I did so,
And heard that instant in an unknown Tongue,
Which yet I understood, articulate sounds,
A loud prophetic blast of harmony,
An Ode, in passion utter'd, which foretold
Destruction to the Children of the Earth,
By deluge now at hand. No sooner ceas'd
The Song, but with calm look, the Arab said
That all was true; that it was even so
As had been spoken; and that he himself
Was going then to bury those two Books:
The one that held acquaintance with the stars,
And wedded man to man by purest bond
Of nature, undisturbed by space or time;
Th' other that was a God, yea many Gods,
Had voices more than all the winds, and was
A joy, a consolation, and a hope.
My friend continued, 'strange as it may seem,
I wonder'd not, although I plainly saw
The one to be a Stone, th' other a Shell,
Nor doubted once but that they both were Books,
Having a perfect faith in all that pass'd
A wish was now ingender'd in my fear
To cleave unto this Man, and I begg'd leave
To share his errand with him. On he pass'd
Not heeding me; I follow'd, and took note
That he look'd often backward with wild look,

4

Grasping his twofold treasure to his side.
—Upon a Dromedary, Lance in rest,
He rode, I keeping pace with him, and now
I fancied that he was the very Knight
Whose Tale Cervantes tells, yet not the Knight,
But was an Arab of the Desart, too;
Of these was neither, and was both at once.
His countenance, meanwhile, grew more disturb'd.
And looking backwards when he look'd, I saw
A glittering light, and ask'd him whence it came.
'It is,' said he, 'the waters of the deep
Gathering upon us,' quickening then his pace
He left me: I call'd after him aloud;
He heeded not; but with his twofold charge
Beneath his arm, before me full in view
I saw him riding o'er the Desart Sands,
With the fleet waters of the drowning world
In chase of him, whereat I wak'd in terror,
And saw the Sea before me; and the Book,
In which I had been reading, at my side.'
                                        Book V. 56–139

Here are three pairs of symbols:
1) The desert and the sea
2) The stone of abstract geometry, and the shell of
   imagination or instinct, which between them offer
   alternative routes of salvation from the anxiety of
   the dreamer, a promise which is not realised.
3) The double-natured hero, half Bedouin, i.e., Ishmael,
   the exile, the Wandering Jew, the Flying Dutchman,
   and half Don Quixote, i.e., the dedicated man, the
   Knight of Faith who would restore the Age of Gold.

5

THE SEA

The second verse of the first chapter of the Book of Genesis runs as follows:

And the earth was without form, and void; and darkness was upon the face of the deep. And the Spirit of God moved upon the face of the waters.

On the first day God said, Let there be light, on the second He

made the firmament, and divided the waters which were under the firmament from the waters which were above the firmament.

And on the third He gathered the waters under the heaven

unto one place, and let the dry land appear; and the gathering together of the waters called he Seas.

Similarly in one of the Greek cosmologies, the beginning of everything was when Eros issued from the egg of Night which floated upon Chaos.

The sea or the great waters, that is, are the symbol for the primordial undifferentiated flux, the substance which became created nature only by having form imposed upon or wedded to it.

The sea, in fact, is that state of barbaric vagueness and disorder out of which civilisation has emerged and into which, unless saved by the effort of gods and men, it is always liable to relapse. It is so little of a friendly symbol that the first thing which the author of the

Book of Revelation notices in his vision of the new heaven and earth at the end of time is that *'there was no more sea.'*

In consequence, though the metaphor of the ship of state or society appears early, it is only employed when society is in peril. The ship ought not to be out of harbor. Thus Horace writes

> *O navis, referent in mare te novi*
> *fluctus. O quid agis! fortiter occupa*
> *portum.*

O ship, new billows are carrying you out to sea. What are you doing? Struggle to reach port.

(Odes I.14)

The ship, then, is only used as a metaphor for society in danger from within or without. When society is normal the image is the City or the Garden. That is where people want and ought to be. As to the sea, the classical authors would have agreed with Marianne Moore. "It is human nature to stand in the middle of a thing; But you cannot stand in the middle of this." A voyage, therefore, is a necessary evil, a crossing of that which separates or estranges. Neither Odysseus nor Jason goes to sea for the sake of the voyage; the former is trying to get home and, if it were not for the enmity of Poseidon, the father of the monster Cyclops, it would be soon over, which is what Odysseus most desires; the latter is trying to capture the Golden Fleece, which is in a distant country, to bring back to his own. If it were

7

nearer and no voyage were necessary, he would be much relieved.*

The state ship that deliberately chooses the high seas is the state in disorder, the Ship of Fools, as in Barclay's adaptation of Brant's *Narrenschiff:*

> Lyke as a myrrour doth represent agayne
> The fourme and fygure of mannes countenaunce
> So in our ship shall he se wrytyn playne
> The fourme and fygure of hys mysgovernaunce.

"What ship is that with so many owners and strange tackle? It is a great vessel. This is the ship of Fools where saileth both spiritual and temporal of every calling some. This ship wanteth a good pilot, the storm, the rocks and the wrecks at hand; all must come to naught for want of good government." †

---

* The Christian conception of time as a divine creation, to be accepted, and not, as in Platonic and Stoic philosophy, ignored, made the journey or pilgrimage a natural symbol for the spiritual life. Similarly the injunction "Whosoever will come after me, let him deny himself, and take up his cross, and follow me" and the distinction between the Kingdom of Heaven and the Kingdom of this world contradicts the classical hope of the perfect *polis*. But, so far as I know, the pilgrimage of the pious soul is never symbolised in early Christian literature by a sea-voyage.

† This looks so similar to the behaviour of the Jumblies, but how differently the reader is expected to feel towards the latter.

> They went to sea in a sieve, they did.
> In a sieve they went to sea:
> In spite of all their friends could say
> On a winter's morn, on a stormy day
> In a sieve they went to sea!
> And when the sieve turned round and round
> And everyone cried, "You'll all be drowned!"
> They called aloud, "Our sieve ain't big,
> But we don't care a button! we don't care a fig!
> In a sieve we'll go to sea."

Similarly in the Anglo-Saxon poems, *The Wanderer* and *The Seafarer*, the mariner is to be pitied rather than admired, for he

> heart weary
> Over ocean streams must for long
> Stir with hands frost-cold sea
> Rove paths of exile.

> No protecting kinsman
> Can bring comfort to the soul in loneliness.
> Full little he thinks who has life's joy
> And dwells in cities and has few disasters,
> Proud and wine-flushed, how I, weary often,
> Must bide my time on the brimming stream.

The sea is no place to be if you can help it, and to try to cross it betrays a rashness bordering on hubris, at which a man's friends should be properly concerned.

> *Nequiquam deus abscidit*
> *prudens Oceano dissociabile*
> *terras si tamen impiae*
> *non tangenda rates transiliunt vada.*

Vain was the purpose of the god in severing the lands by the estranging sea, if in spite of him our impious ships dash across the depths he meant should never be touched.

(Horace Odes I. 3)

There is a famous passage in the 26th canto of Dante's *Inferno* which is interesting not only for its beauty, but because the legend of Ulysses' last voyage appears to be Dante's own invention.

Ulysses is in Hell for having been an Evil Counsellor. Dante begins rather mysteriously

I sorrowed then, and sorrow now again when I direct my memory to what I saw; and curb my genius more than I am wont lest it run where Virtue guides it not.

Ulysses in describing his end says: "Neither fondness for my son nor reverence for my aged father, nor the due love that should have cheered Penelope could conquer in me the ardor that I had to gain experience of the world, of human vice and worth." To his fellow-mariners he had argued: "Consider your origin: ye were not formed to live like brutes but to follow virtue and knowledge."

Ulysses behaves like the typical Romantic Marine Hero, which in Tennyson's version of the same story he, indeed, becomes, but to Dante, clearly, his action was not only reprehensible but, as the last sentence shows, essentially the original sin of Adam, and in his speech to his fellows, he is once more, as earlier at Troy, the Evil Counsellor whose words echo the words of the Serpent to Eve. Perhaps, too, Dante's opening remarks indicate that the same temptation to the concupiscence of curiosity was his own.

The handling of the symbols of sea and storm by Shakespeare provides us with a bridge between what, for convenience, one may call the classic attitude and the romantic. The subject has been so exhaustively

10

and sensitively studied by Mr. Wilson Knight in *The Shakesperian Tempest* * as to make much further comment superfluous. As Wilson Knight demonstrates, in most of Shakespeare's plays there are two antithetical symbolic clusters. On the one hand tempests, rough beasts, comets, diseases, malice domestic and private vice, that is, the world of conflict and disorder; on the other hand music, flowers, birds, precious stones and marriage, the world of reconciliation and order. In the earlier plays the stormy sea is more purely negative, a reflection of human conflict or the fatal mischance which provides evil with its opportunity (e.g. *Othello*). In the last plays, *Pericles*, *The Winter's Tale*, *The Tempest*, however, not only do the sea and the sea voyage play a much more important role, but also a different one. The sea becomes the place of purgatorial suffering: through separation and apparent loss, the characters disordered by passion are brought to their senses and the world of music and marriage is made possible. There is, however, one extremely important difference in the relation of the actors to the sea from that which our period exhibits, namely, that the putting to sea, the wandering is never *voluntarily* entered upon as a pleasure. It is a pain which must be accepted as cure, the death that leads to rebirth, in order that the abiding city may be built. Deliberately to seek the exile is still folly. Thus, in *The Winter's Tale* the good old counsellor Camillo advises the young lovers

* Oxford Press, 1932

Florizel and Perdita to enlist the help of Leontes rather than to elope.

> A course more promising
> Than a wild dedication of yourselves
> To unpath'd waters, undream'd shores, most certain
> To miseries enough: no hope to help you,
> But as you shake off one to take another;
> Nothing so certain as your anchors, who
> Do their best office, if they can but stay you
> Where you'll be loath to be.
>
> *The Winter's Tale* IV 4

The distinctive new notes in the Romantic attitude are as follows.

1) To leave the land and the city is the desire of every man of sensibility and honor.
2) The sea is the real situation and the voyage is the true condition of man.

"The port we sail from is far astern and, though far out of sight of land, for ages and ages we continue to sail with sealed orders and our last destination remains a secret to ourselves and our officers. And yet our final haven was predestined ere we stepped from the stocks of creation. Let us not give ear to the superstitious gun-deck gossip about whither we may be gliding for, as yet, not a soul on board of us knows—not even the commodore himself—assuredly not the chaplain—even our professors' scientific surmisings are vain. On that point, the smallest cabin boy is as wise as the captain."

(White Jacket)

3) The sea is where the decisive events, the moments of eternal choice, of temptation, fall, and redemption occur. The shore life is always trivial.

4) An abiding destination is unknown even if it may exist: a lasting relationship is not possible nor even to be desired.

> *Les vrais voyageurs sont ceux-là seuls qui partent*
> *Pour partir; coeurs légers, semblables aux ballons,*
> *De leur fatalité jamais ils ne s'écartent,*
> *Et, sans savoir pourquoi, disent toujours: Allons!*
> Baudelaire (*Le Voyage*)

THE DESERT

Like the sea, the desert is the nucleus of a cluster of traditional associations.

1) It is the place where the water of life is lacking, the valley of dry bones in Ezekiel's vision.

2) It may be so by nature, i.e., the wilderness which lies *outside* the fertile place or city. As such, it is the place where nobody desires by nature to be. Either one is compelled by others to go there because one is a criminal outlaw or a scapegoat (e.g. Cain, Ishmael), or one chooses to withdraw from the city in order to be alone. This withdrawal may be temporary, a period of self-examination and purification in order to return to the city with a true knowledge of one's mission and the strength to carry it out (e.g. Jesus' forty days in the wilderness), or it may be permanent, a final rejection of the wicked

13

city of this world, a dying to the life of the flesh and an assumption of a life devoted wholly to spiritual contemplation and prayer (e.g. the Thebaid).

3) The natural desert is therefore at once the place of punishment for those rejected by the good city because they are evil, and the place of purgation for those who reject the evil city because they desire to become good. In the first case the desert image is primarily related to the idea of justice, i.e., the desert is the place outside the law. As such it may be the home of the dragon or any lawless power which is hostile to the city and so be the place out into which the hero must venture in order to deliver the city from danger. An elaboration of this is the myth of the treasure in the desert guarded by the dragon. This treasure belongs by right to the city and has either been stolen by force or lost through the city's own sin. The hero then performs a double task. He delivers the city from danger and restores the precious life-giving object to its rightful owners.

In the second case, when the desert is the purgative place, the image is primarily associated with the idea of chastity and humility. It is the place where there are no beautiful bodies or comfortable beds or stimulating food and drink or admiration. The temptations of the desert are therefore either sexual mirages raised by the devil to make the hermit nostalgic for his old life or the more subtle temptations of pride when the devil appears in his own form.

14

4) The natural wilderness may lie not only outside the city but also *between* one city and another, i.e., be the place to be crossed, in which case the image is associated with the idea of vocation. Only the individual or community with the faith and courage which can dare, endure, and survive its trials is worthy to enter into the promised land of the New Life.

5) Lastly, the desert may not be barren by nature but as the consequence of a historical catastrophe. The once-fertile city has become, through the malevolence of others or its own sin, the waste land. In this case it is the opportunity for the stranger hero who comes from elsewhere to discover the cause of the disaster, destroy or heal it and become the rebuilder of the city and, in most cases, its new ruler.

THE ROMANTIC SEA AND THE ROMANTIC DESERT

Resemblances

1) Both are the wilderness, i.e., the place where there is no community, just or unjust, and no historical change for better or for worse.

2) Therefore the individual in either is free from both the evils and the responsibilities of communal life. Thus Byron writes of the ocean:

> Man marks the earth with ruin—his control
> Stops with the shore.
>
> (*Childe Harold*)

15

And Captain Nemo, the commander of the submarine *Nautilus* in *Twenty Thousand Leagues Under the Sea*, cries:

"The sea does not belong to despots. Upon its surface men can still exercise unjust laws, fight, tear one another to pieces, and be carried away with terrestrial horrors. But at thirty feet below its level, their reign ceases, their influence is quenched, and their power disappears. Ah, sir; live, live in the bosom of the waters. There only is independence. There I recognize no master's voice. There I am free."

And so Carmen tempts Don José to leave the fertile plain for the barren lawless mountains.

> *Tu n'y dépendrais de personne.*
> *Point d'officier à qui tu doives obéir*
> *Et point de retraite qui sonne*
> *Pour dire à l'amoureux qu'il est temps de partir.*

Both, in fact, are characterised by the absence of limitations, of '*les arrêts de la vie*,' the Ocean-chart that the Bellman bought describes them well.

"What's the good of Mercator's North Poles and Equators,
  Tropics, Zones, and Meridian Lines?"
So the Bellman would cry: and the crew would reply
  "They are merely conventional signs!

"Other maps are such shapes, with their islands and capes!
  But we've got our brave Captain to thank"
(So the crew would protest) "that he's bought *us* the best—
  A perfect and absolute blank!"

Le ciel ouvert
La vie errante
Pour pays l'univers
Et pour loi sa volonté
Et surtout la chose enivrante
La liberté.

Meilhac and Halévy (*Carmen*)

3) But precisely because they are free places, they are also lonely places of alienation, and the individual who finds himself there, whether by choice or fate, must from time to time, rightly or wrongly, be visited by desperate longings for home and company. So Ishmael, however he may convince himself that "in landlessness alone resides highest truth, shoreless, indefinite as God—so better is it to perish in that lonely infinite than be ingloriously dashed upon the lea, even if that were safety," nevertheless, as he squeezes out the whale sperm with his hands, he is compelled to reflect that "Happiness is not in the intellect or the fancy—but in the wife, the heart, the bed, the table, the saddle, the fireside, the country." So Ahab, on that final beautiful day before his encounter with Moby Dick, softens and calls despairingly to Starbuck: "Stand close to me, Starbuck; let me look into a human eye; it is better than to gaze into sea or sky; better than to gaze upon God. By the green land; by the bright hearthstone! this is the magic glass, man; I see my wife and my child in thine eye. . . . It is a mild, mild wind, and a mild-looking meadow; they have been making hay some-

17

where under the slopes of the Andes, Starbuck, and the mowers are sleeping among the new-mown hay." Even that most passionate Don Quixote of absolute freedom, the Rimbaud of *Bateau Ivre*, is forced to confess

> *Je regrette l'Europe aux anciens parapets*

and to remember nostalgically a time of a more restricted loneliness when on a black cold pond

> *Un enfant accroupi, plein de tristesse, lâche*
> *Un bateau frêle comme un papillon de mai.*

And so too in his moment of greatest anguish when the Ancient Mariner is

> Alone, alone, all, all alone
> Alone on a wide wide sea!

he looks up yearningly to the moon and the stars and the blue sky which, says the Gloss, "belongs to them, and is their appointed rest, and their native country and their own natural homes." And when he repents, and the ship begins to move again, he is refreshed by the sound of the sails

> A noise like of a hidden brook
> In the leafy month of June,
> That to the sleeping woods all night
> Singeth a quiet tune.

Differences

As places of freedom and solitude the sea and the desert are symbolically the same. In other respects, however, they are opposites. E.g. the desert is the dried-up place, i.e., the place where life has ended, the Omega of temporal existence. Its first most obvious characteristic is that nothing moves; the second is that everything is surface and exposed. No soil, no hidden spring. The sea, on the other hand, is the Alpha of existence, the symbol of potentiality.

> Thy shores are empires, changed in all save thee—
> Assyria, Greece, Rome, Carthage, what are they?
> Thy waters wash'd them power while they were free,
> And many a tyrant since; their shores obey
> The stranger, slave, or savage; their decay
> Has dried up realms to deserts:—not so thou;—
> Unchangeable, save to thy wild waves' play,
> Time notes no wrinkle on thine azure brow:
> Such as creation's dawn beheld, thou rollest now.
>
> (*Childe Harold* Canto IV)

Its first most obvious characteristic is its perpetual motion, the violence of wave as tempest; its power may be destructive, but unlike that of the desert, it is positive. Its second is the teeming life that lies hidden below the surface which, however dreadful, is greater than the visible: "As this appalling ocean surrounds the verdant land, so in the soul of man there lies one insular Tahiti, full of peace and joy, but encompassed by all the horror of the half-known life."(*Moby Dick*)

The sea, then, is the symbol of primitive potential power as contrasted with the desert of actualised triviality, of living barbarism versus lifeless decadence.

19

THE OASIS AND THE HAPPY ISLAND

The sea and the desert are related to the city as its symbolic opposites. There is a third image, in the case of the sea the happy island and in the case of the desert the oasis or rose garden, which stands related to both. It is like the city in that it is an enclosed place of safety and like the sea-desert in that it is a solitary or private place from which the general public are excluded and where the writ of the law does not run. The primary idea with which the garden-island image is associated is, therefore, neither justice nor chastity but innocence; it is the earthly paradise where there is no conflict between natural desire and moral duty.

Thus Pindar sings in the second Olympian of the land of the Hyperboreans

> In sunshine ever fair
> Abide the Good and all their nights and days
> An equal splendour wear.
> And never as of old with thankless toil
> For their poor empty needs they vex the soil
>   And plough the watery seas
> But dwelling with the glorious gods in ease
>   A tearless life they pass.

And Euripides in *Hippolytus*

> To the strand of the Daughters of the sunset,
>   The apple tree, the singing and the gold;
> Where the mariner must stay him from his onset
>   And the red wave is tranquil as of old;
>   Yea beyond that Pillar of the End
>   That Atlas guardeth, would I wend.

20

And the same nostalgia is common among the romantics, for *l'innocent paradis, plein de plaisirs furtifs*, where

> *tout n'est qu'ordre et beauté*
> *Luxe, calme et volupté.*

This image, in its turn, has two possibilities. Either it is the real earthly paradise, in which case it is a place of temporary refreshment for the exhausted hero, a foretaste of rewards to come or the final goal and reward itself, where the beloved and the blessed society are waiting to receive him into their select company; or it is a magical garden, an illusion caused by black magic to tempt the hero to abandon his quest, and which, when the spell is broken, is seen to be really the desert of barren rock, or a place of horror like Calypso's island, Klingsor's garden, or the isle of Venus.*

---

* An interesting example of the tempting island imagery because of the unusual twist given to it is Tennyson's *Voyage of Maeldune*. In this poem there are nine islands which I associate, perhaps rather arbitrarily, with certain ideas as follows.

The Silent Isle	Introversion
The Shouting Isle	Extroversion
The Isle of Flowers but no Fruits	Art
The Isle of Fruits	Science
The Isle of Fire	Materialism
The Isle under the Sea	Mysticism
The Beauteous Isle	Leisure
The Isle of Witches	Sex
The Isle of Double Towers	Religious and Political Fanaticism

Maeldune's crew, when they first sight these islands, expect to enjoy themselves, i.e., they expect to be tempted to stay and be untrue to

THE ROMANTIC OASIS-ISLAND

The image of the happy Prelapsarian Place appears often enough in Romantic literature but charged usually with a hopeless nostalgia. The examples which the romantic actually encounters turn out to be mirages or disappointing and dangerous deserts like the *Encantadas* of which Melville writes:

"Change never comes, neither the change of seasons nor of sorrows. No voice, no low, no howl is heard: the chief sound of life here is a hiss. In no world but a fallen one could such lands exist."

Where the population consists of

Men	0
Ant-eaters	Unknown
Man-haters	Unknown
Lizards	500,000
Snakes	500,000
Spiders	10,000,000
Salamanders	Unknown
Devils	Do. Do.

Eldorado turns out to be a reef, the island of Cythera is

un terrain des plus maigres,
Un désert rocailleux troublé par des cris aigres
Baudelaire (*Voyage à Cythère*)

their mission, which is one of vengeance. What happens, however, is that the islands turn out to be places of danger which make them kill each other or commit suicide, i.e., turn their aggressive feelings away from the absent object against themselves. Thus the islands become the means by which Maeldune and they are taught through suffering from hate that hate is hateful.

When at last they landed on the shore where the Snarks were to be found

> the crew were not pleased with the view
> Which consisted of chasms and crags.

And the natural surroundings of Lady Jingly Jones are in keeping with her lovelorn condition

> On that coast of Coromandel
> In his jug without a handle
> Still she weeps and still she moans,
> On that little heap of stones.

The tempestuous liquid sea is dangerous enough but when it approaches the condition of the solid desert it is worse. E.g. the sand-bank of the Kentish Knock in *The Wreck of the Deutschland* and the iceberg in Melville's poem

> Hard Berg (methought), so cold, so vast,
> With mortal damps self-overcast;
> Exhaling still thy dankish breath—
> Adrift dissolving, bound for death;
> Though lumpish thou, a lumbering one—
> A lumbering lubbard loitering slow,
> Impingers rue thee and go down
> Sounding thy precipice below,
> Nor stir the slimy slug that sprawls
> Along thy dead indifference of walls.

23

And the Ancient Mariner's punishment begins when the sea becomes a counterfeit desert.

> Day after day, day after day,
> We stuck, nor breath nor motion;
> As idle as a painted ship
> Upon a painted ocean.
>
> Water, water, everywhere,
> And all the boards did shrink;
> Water, water, everywhere,
> Nor any drop to drink.
>
> The very deep did rot: O Christ!
> That ever this should be!
> Yea, slimy things did crawl with legs
> Upon the slimy sea.

To the romantic, that is, childhood is over, its island is astern, and there is no other. The only possible place of peace now lies under the waters.

"Where lies the final harbor whence we unmoor no more? Where is the foundling's father hidden? Our souls are like those orphans whose unwedded mothers die in bearing them: the secret of our paternity lies in their grave, and we must there to learn it."

(Moby Dick)

The images of the Just City, of the civilised landscape protected by the Madonna, the *"Fior, frondi, ombre,*

24

antri, onde, aure soavi" which look at us from so many Italian paintings, and of the rose garden or island of the blessed, are lacking in Romantic literature because the Romantic writers no longer believe in their existence. What exists is the Trivial Unhappy Unjust City, the desert of the average from which the only escape is to the wild, lonely, but still vital sea. The Desert has become, in fact, an image of modern civilisation in which innocence and the individual are alike destroyed.

THE LEVEL DESERT

None of the writers we are discussing had much good to say for laissez-faire democracy. Rimbaud's poem on that subject expresses an attitude shared by most of them.

DEMOCRACY

The flag is in keeping with the unclean landscape, and our jargon drowns the sound of the drums.

At certain centres we will encourage the most cynical prostitution. We will crush logical rebellion.

Let us go to dusty and exhausted countries—put ourselves at the service of monstrous industrial or military exploitations.

"To our next meeting—here—no matter where!"

Conscripts of good intentions we shall have a ferocious philosophy. Dunces shall be devotees of knowledge, sybarites

25

enthusiasts for comfort; and for this busy world there shall be dissolution.

This is real progress! Forward! March!

(*Les Illuminations*)

And Baudelaire foresaw a democratic future when "the son will run away from the family not at eighteen but at twelve, emancipated by his gluttonous precocity; he will fly, not to seek heroic adventures, not to deliver a beautiful prisoner from a tower, not to immortalize a garret with sublime thoughts, but to found a business, to enrich himself and to compete with his infamous papa" and the daughter, "with an infantile wantonness, will dream in her cradle that she sells herself for a million."

(*Fusées*)

They did not feel like this because they disbelieved in individual freedom but precisely because, passionately believing in it, they saw urban democracy as they knew it, destroying the heroic individual and turning him into a cypher of the crowd, or a mechanical cogwheel in an impersonal machine.

What Baudelaire stigmatises as *l'esprit belge*, what Jack Chase means when he says, "let us hate the public and cleave to the people," what Lear means by They in such a limerick as

> There was an old man of Whitehaven
> Who danced a quadrille with a raven

They said: It's absurd
To encourage this bird
So they smashed that old man of Whitehaven.

is dealt with most fully by Kierkegaard:

"The man who has no opinion of an event at the actual moment accepts the opinion of the majority, or if he is quarrelsome, of the minority. But it must be remembered that both majority and minority are real people, and that is why the individual is assisted by adhering to them. A public, on the contrary, is an abstraction . . . A public is neither a nation, nor a generation, nor a community, nor these particular men, for all these are only what they are through the concrete; no single person who belongs to the public makes a real commitment; for some hours of the day, perhaps, he belongs to the public—at moments when he is nothing else, since when he is really what he is he does not form part of the public. Made up of such individuals, of individuals at the moments when they are nothing, a public is a kind of gigantic something, an abstract and deserted void which is everything and nothing."

(Thoughts on the Present Age)

So, too, Wordsworth saw the London crowds:

The slaves unrespited of low pursuits,
Living amid the same perpetual flow
Of trivial objects, melted and reduced
To one identity, by differences
That have no law, no meaning, and no end.
(Prelude VII 700–704)

27

Again, although it has struck many readers as unjust, Coleridge was imaginatively correct in allowing all the companions of the Ancient Mariner to die. The latter has sinned by shooting the Albatross, but the sin is a personal act for which he can suffer and repent. The rest of the crew react collectively as a crowd, not as persons. First they blame him because they think he has killed the bird that made the breeze to blow, then they praise him for having killed the bird that brought the fog and mist, and then when the ship is becalmed, they turn on him again and hang the albatross around his neck. That is to say, they are an irresponsible crowd and since, as such, they can take no part in the Mariner's personal repentance, they must die to be got out of the way.

THE MECHANISED DESERT

If, in the overlarge, industrialised cities against which the romantic poets protest, the masses during their hours of leisure lack any real common bond of love or commitment and turn into crowds, in their working hours they tend to become mere instruments of their particular function, to have no existence over and above what they do to earn their living.

With the exception of the Beaver, the Bellman's crew in *The Hunting of the Snark* have no names, only jobs, Boots, Maker of Bonnets and Hoods, Barrister, Broker, Billiard Marker, Banker, Butcher, and Baker (the reason why the last is said to have forgotten his name, we shall consider later). It is not that they are passionate about these jobs, dedicated to them by a personal choice, no, these are just what they happen to do. The best portrait of this depersonalised technician is the Carpenter of the *Pequod*, "a strict abstract" who "works by a deaf and dumb spontaneous literal process, a pure manipulator: his brain, if he had ever had one, must have early oozed along with the muscles of his fingers." He is a solitary who has no relationships with human beings, only with wood and his tools, without being a simple individual. Then he continually talks to himself, but is incapable of a real dialogue of self with self, only a meaningless stream of free associations set off by the actions of his fingers, soliloquising "like the whirring wheel—to keep himself awake."

Drat the file, and drat the bone! That is hard which should be soft, and that is soft which should be hard. So we go, who file old jaws and shinbones. Let's try another. Aye, now, this works better (*sneezes*). Halloa, this bone dust is (*sneezes*)—why it's (*sneezes*)—yes, it's (*sneezes*)—bless my soul, it won't let me speak! This is what an old fellow gets now for working in dead lumber. Saw a live tree, and you don't get this dust; amputate a live bone, and you don't get it (*sneezes*). Come, come, you old Smut, there, bear a hand, and let's have that ferule and buckle-screw; I'll be ready for them presently. Lucky now (*sneezes*) there's no knee-joint to make; that might puzzle a little; but a mere shinbone—why it's easy as making hop-poles; only I should like to put a good finish on. Time, time; if I but only had the time, I could turn him out as neat a leg now as ever scraped to a lady in a parlor . . . There!

before I saw it off, now, I must call his old Mogulship, and see whether the length will be all right; too short, if anything, I guess. Ha! that's the heel; we are in luck; here he comes, or it's somebody else, that's certain.

(*Moby Dick.* Chapter cviii)

What has happened, in fact, is the disappearance of a true community, i.e., a group of rational beings associated on the basis of a common love. Societies still exist, i.e., organisations of talents for the sake of a given function. Communities and societies are not identical, i.e., a cello player in a string quartet, who hates music but plays because he must eat and playing the cello is all he knows, is a member of a society; he is not a member of the community of music lovers, but in a healthy culture societies exist as differentiated units inside a common community.

In a society, where the structure and relation of its members to each other is determined by the function for which the society exists and not by their personal choice, the whole is more real than the sum of its parts. In a community, on the other hand, which is determined by the subjective verbs Love or Believe, *I* always precedes *We*. In a closed traditional community this fact is hidden, because the *I* is only potential. The believer by tradition is unconscious of any alternative to his belief—he has only heard of one kind of snark, and therefore cannot doubt. The further civilisation moves towards the open condition in which each man is conscious that there are snarks that have feathers and bite and snarks that have whiskers and scratch, the sharper becomes the alternative: *either* personal choice and through the sum of such choices an actual community *or* the annihilation of personality and the dissolution of community into crowds.

A cartoon by Charles Addams which appeared some years ago in *The New Yorker* illustrates admirably the urban situation in which individuality is lost. It shows a residential street in New York. Along the pavement a motionless line of spectators is staring at a little man with an umbrella engaged in a life-and-death struggle with a large octopus which has emerged from a manhole in the middle of the street. Behind the crowd two men with brief-cases are walking along without bothering to turn their heads and one is saying to the other: "It doesn't take much to collect a crowd in New York."

The cartoon contains three groups:

1) The majority crowd, no member of which dares move unless the rest do so, so that all remain passive spectators and not one steps out to help the man in trouble and, by doing so, to become an individual.

2) The minority crowd who are, indeed, acting (they are walking, not standing still) but whose actions and feelings are negatively conditioned by the majority, i.e., what they do is not their personal choice, but whatever it may be that the majority does *not* do.

3) The single man struggling with the octopus. He is a real individual, yet even with him, the question arises: "Would he be standing out there in the street

31

by himself if the octopus had not attacked him?"
i.e., if he had not been compelled by a fate outside
his personal control to become the exceptional individual. There is even a suggestion about his bourgeois umbrella of a magician's wand. Could it be
possible that, desiring to become an individual yet
unable to do so by himself, he has conjured up a
monster from the depths of the sea to break the
spell of reflection, and free him from being just a
member of the crowd?

It is not only the little man in the bowler hat, however, who is in danger of loss of individuality. As
Nietzsche perceived, the brilliant scholarly mind is, in
modern civilisation, even more threatened.

However gratefully one may welcome the objective spirit—
and who has not been sick to death of all subjectivity and its
confounded *ipsisimosity*—in the end, however, one must learn
caution, even with regard to one's gratitude, and put a stop
to the exaggeration with which the unselfing and deperson-
alising of the spirit has recently been celebrated, as if it were
the goal in itself, as if it were a salvation and glorification—
as is especially accustomed to happen in the pessimist school,
which has also in its turn good reasons for paying the highest
honours to "disinterested knowledge." The objective man,
who no longer curses and scolds like the pessimist, the *ideal*
man of learning in whom the scientific instinct blossoms forth
fully after a thousand complete and partial failures, is surely
one of the most costly instruments that exist, but his place is
in the hand of one who is more powerful. He is only an instru-
ment—we may say he is a *mirror*, he is no "purpose in him-

self." The objective man is in truth a mirror. Accustomed to prostration before everything that wants to be known, with such desires only as knowing and reflecting imply—he waits until something comes, and then expands himself sensitively, so that even the lightest footsteps and gliding past of spiritual beings may not be lost on his surface and film. Whatever "personality" he still possesses seems to him accidental, arbitrary, or still oftener disturbing; so much has he come to regard himself as the passage and reflection of outside forms and events. He calls up the recollection of "himself" with an effort. He readily confounds himself with other people, he makes mistakes with regard to his own needs, and here only is he unrefined and negligent. Perhaps he is troubled about the health, or the pettiness and confined atmosphere of wife and friend, or the lack of companions and society—and indeed, he sets himself to reflect on his suffering, but in vain! His thoughts already rove away to the *more general* case, and tomorrow he knows as little as he knew yesterday how to help himself. He does not now take himself seriously and devote time to himself: he is serene, *not* from lack of troubles, but from lack of capacity for grasping and dealing with *his* trouble. The habitual complaisance with respect to all objects and experiences, the radiant and impartial hospitality with which he receives everything that comes his way, his habit of inconsiderate good nature, of dangerous indifference to Yea and Nay . . . Should one wish Love or Hatred from him— and I mean Love and Hatred as God, woman and animal understand them, he will do what he can, and furnish what he can. But one must not be surprised if it should not be much— if he should show himself just at this point to be false, fragile, and rather *un tour de force*, a slight ostentation and exaggeration. He is only genuine so far as he can be objective;

33

only in his serene totality is he still "nature" and "natural." His mirroring and eternally self-polishing soul no longer knows how to affirm, no longer how to deny; he does not command; neither does he destroy. "Je ne méprise presque rien"—he says with Leibnitz: let us not overlook nor undervalue the *presque!*

(*Beyond Good and Evil*)

If a community so dissolves, the societies, which remain so long as human beings wish to remain alive, must, left to themselves, grow more and more mechanical. And such real individuals as are left must become Ishmaels, "isolatoes, not acknowledging the common continent of men, but each isolatoe living in a separate continent of his own;" Hamlet is at the mercy of reflection and melancholia.

What it feels like to be such an isolatoe, who cannot take the crowd way and become a grain of the desert sand, but is left standing there alone in the wide waste, is described similarly by most of them.

Thus Coleridge:

> A grief without a pang, void, dark, and drear,
>   A stifled, drowsy, unimpassioned grief,
>   Which finds no natural outlet, no relief,
>   In word, or sigh, or tear—
> O Lady! in this wan and heartless mood,
> To other thoughts by yonder throstle wooed,
>   All this long eve, so balmy and serene,
> Have I been gazing on the western sky,
>   And its peculiar tint of yellow green:
> And still I gaze—and with how blank an eye!

34

And those thin clouds above, in flakes and bars,
That give away their motion to the stars;
Those stars, that glide behind them or between,
Now sparkling, now bedimmed, but always seen:
Yon crescent Moon, as fixed as if it grew
In its own cloudless, starless lake of blue,
I see them all so excellently fair,
I see, not feel, how beautiful they are!

> (*Dejection*)

Thus Baudelaire:

Rien n'égale en longueur les boiteuses journées
Quand sous les lourds flocons des neigeuses années
L'ennui, fruit de la morne incuriosité,
Prend les proportions de l'immortalité.

—Désormais tu n'es plus, o matière vivante!
Qu'un granit entouré d'une vague épouvante,
Assoupi dans le fond d'un Sahara brumeux!
Un vieux sphinx ignoré du monde insoucieux,
Oublié sur la carte, et dont l'humeur farouche
Ne chante qu'aux rayons du soleil qui se couche!

> (*Spleen*)

Thus Melville:

It is a damp drizzly November in my soul;—I find myself
involuntarily pausing before coffin warehouses, and bringing
up the rear of every funeral I meet . . . it requires a strong
moral principle to prevent me from deliberately stepping into
the street, and methodically knocking people's hats off.

> (*Moby Dick*. Chapter i)

35

And Mallarmé in a sentence:

La chair est triste, hélas! et j'ai lu tous les livres.

The grand explanatory image of this condition is of course Dürer's *Melancholia*. She sits unable to sleep and yet unable to work, surrounded by unfinished works and unused tools, the potential fragments of the city which she has the knowledge but not the will to build, tormented by a batlike creature with a board, bearing figures, and, behind her, a dark sea, a rainbow and a comet.

What is the cause of her suffering? That, surrounded by every possibility, she cannot find within herself or without the necessity to realise one rather than another. Urban society is, like the desert, a place without limits. The city walls of tradition, mythos and cultus have crumbled. There is no direction in which Ishmael is forbidden or forcibly prevented from moving. The only outside "necessities" are the random winds of fashion or the lifeless chains of a meaningless job, which, so long as he remains an individual, he can and will reject. At the same time, however, he fails to find a necessity within himself to take their place. So he must take drastic measures and go down to the waters, though in a very different sense from those of which St. John of the Cross speaks:

> *Y el cerco sosegaba*
> *Y la caballeria*
> *A vista de las aguas descendia*

The siege was intermitted and the cavalry dismounted at the sight of the waters.

> *Song of the Soul and the Bridegroom*

For the waters to which Ishmael goes are bitter and medicinal.

> God help me! save I take my part
>   Of danger on the roaring sea,
> A devil rises in my heart
>   Far worse than any death to me.
>
> (Tennyson *The Sailor Boy*)

Fleeing to the ship where "the sons of adversity meet the children of calamity and the children of calamity meet the offspring of sin," yet at least, facing a common death, he and they are bound into a true community, so unlike the landsmen children of Abel of whom Baudelaire says

> *Race d'Abel tu crois et broutes*
> *Comme les punaises des bois.*

And then out to sea, for there in the ocean wastes, the Paternal Power may still be felt though but as dreadful tempest, and there still dwells the Mother-Goddess though she appear but in her most malignant aspects, as the castrating white whale to Ahab, as the Life-in-Death to the Ancient Mariner

> Her lips were red, her looks were free
> Her locks were yellow as gold:
> Her skin was white as leprosy.

37

as the ghoul Ice-maiden to Gordon Pym.

"And now we rushed into the embrace of the cataract where a chasm threw itself open to receive us. But there arose in our pathway a shrouded human figure, very far larger in its proportions than any dweller among men. And the hue of the skin of the figure was of the perfect whiteness of snow."

Or, worst of all, the dreadful Boojum of Nothingness. Shipwreck is probable, but at least it will be a positive Death.

> *Je partirai! steamer balançant ta mâture*
> *Lève l'ancre pour une exotique nature!*
> *Un Ennui, désolé par les cruels espoirs,*
> *Croit encore à l'adieu suprême des mouchoirs!*
> *Et, peut-être, les mâts, invitant les orages,*
> *Sont-ils de ceux qu'un vent penche sur les naufrages*
> *Perdus, sans mâts, sans mâts, ni fertiles îlots . . .*
> *Mais, ô mon coeur, entends les chants des matelots.*
>
> (Mallarmé)

TWO

The Stone and the Shell

wwwwwwww

"The Non-Limited is the original material of existing things; further, the source from which existing things derive their existence is also that to which they return at their destruction, according to necessity; for they give justice and make reparation to one another for their injustice, according to the arrangement of Time."

ANAXIMANDER OF MILETUS.

"The nature of Number and Harmony admits of no Falsehood; for this is unrelated to them. Falsehood and Envy belong to the nature of the Non-Limited and the Unintelligent and the Irrational."

PHILOLAUS OF TARENTUM.

THE DESERT KNIGHT OF WORDSWORTH'S DREAM WAS
hurrying away to hide two treasures, a stone and a shell,
and the poet is quite explicit as to their significance.
The stone is geometric truth, which holds acquaintance
with the stars and weds man to man

> "by purest bond
> Of nature undisturbed by space or time."

For it is An image, not unworthy of the one
Surpassing life which out of space and time
Nor touched by weltering of passion is
And has the name of God.

And the shell is Poetic Truth, the truth built by

> passion which itself
> Is highest reason in a soul sublime

for it is a god, yea many gods
has voices more than all the winds
and is a joy, a consolation and a hope

Further he says quite definitely that the shell is of more
worth than the stone.

As symbolic object, the stone is related to the desert,

40

which like the Ancient Mariner's situation is a becalmed
state when the distress is caused by lack of passion, good
or bad, and the shell is related to the sea, to powers, that
is, which, though preferable to aridity, are nevertheless
more dangerous; the shell is a consolation yet what it
says is a prophecy of destruction by the weltering flood;
and only a sublime soul can ride the storm.

The poet himself indeed is often endangered by his
shell, and in the Seventh Book Wordsworth speaks of
his interest in geometry in the following terms

> Mighty is the charm
> Of these abstractions to a mind beset
> With images and haunted by itself

and then compares himself with a shipwrecked mariner
who passed the time on a desert island drawing dia-
grams with a stick, escaping from the distress of his
corporal situation into

> an independent world
> Created out of pure intelligence.

The Whale of Truth is "for salamander giants only
to encounter," and thinking can be as dangerous as
feeling. He who is merely a provincial, one of those
"romantic, melancholy, and absent-minded young men,
disgusted with the carking cares of earth" must be-
ware of gazing too long at the sea or the fire, for even
as he takes "the mystic ocean at his feet for the visible
image of that deep, blue, bottomless soul pervading

41

mankind and nature" he is hovering over Descartian vortices

and perhaps at midday, in the fairest weather, with one half-throttled shriek you drop through that transparent air into the summer sea, no more to rise for ever,

(Moby Dick. Chapter xxxv)

the fate, for instance, of the timid child Pip, who against his own will was cast into the sea, saw "God's foot upon the treadle of the loom" and went mad, the fate of the over-sensitive Cowper:

> No voice divine the storm allay'd,
>   No light propitious shone,
> When, snatched from all effectual aid,
>   We perished, each alone:
> But I beneath a rougher sea
> And whelmed in deeper gulphs than he.
> *(The Castaway)*

When the preself-conscious savage Tashtego falls into the cistern of the sperm-whale head and is nearly drowned, Ishmael remarks, "How many, think ye, have likewise fallen into Plato's honey head, and sweetly perished there?" Even the hero may perish: the baker for all his courage vanishes away when he encounters the Boojum; and tough Baudelaire notes in his journal, "I have cultivated my hysteria with delight and terror. Now I suffer continually from vertigo, and today, the 23rd of January 1862, I have received a singular warning. I have felt the wind of the wing of madness pass over me."

THE STONE, THE SHELL AND
THE CITY

In Wordsworth's dream, then, as in all dreams, there are a number of ambiguities.

1) The stone and the shell are alike in that they both signify Truth. They are also opposites. The stone is valuable because it stands for freedom from disorder and passion. The shell is valuable because it stands for life-giving power. Incidentally, also, the stone stands for the Divine Unity, the shell for the Divine Multiplicity.

2) Both are the means through which the True City is built. Men become brothers through the recognition of a common truth in their several minds, and through the experience of a common hope and joy in their several hearts. But at the same time both are dangers to the city. The truths of abstraction are unrelated to the historical reality of the human moment and distract from the historical task. The truths of feeling may overwhelm individual identity and social order in an anarchic deluge.

THE POLEMICAL SITUATION OF
ROMANTICISM

For every individual the present moment is a polemical situation, and his battle is always on two fronts: he has to fight against his own past, not only his personal past but also those elements in the previous generation with which he is personally involved—in the case of a poet, for instance, the poetic tradition and attitudes of the preceding generation—and simultaneously he has to fight against the present of others, who are a threat to him, against the beliefs and attitudes of the society in which he lives which are hostile to his conception of art. In order to plunge straight away into this question, let us take a few statements by that highly polemical writer William Blake.

"Cowper came to me and said: O that I were insane always. . . . Can you not make me truly insane? I will never rest till I am so. O that in the bosom of God I was hid. You claim health and yet are as mad as any of us all . . . mad as a refuge from unbelief—from Bacon, Newton and Locke."

> Mock on, Mock on Voltaire, Rousseau:
> Mock on, Mock on: 'tis all in vain!
> You throw the sand against the wind,
> And the wind blows it back again. . . .

> The Atoms of Democritus
> And Newton's Particles of light
> Are sands upon the Red sea shore
> Where Israel's tents do shine so bright.

"The bounded is loathed by its possessor. The same dull round, even of a universe, would soon become a mill with complicated wheels."

"Doctor Thornton's Tory Translation, Translated out of its disguise in the Classical & Scotch languages into the vulgar English.

"Our Father Augustus Caesar, who art in these thy Substantial Astronomical Telescopic Heavens, Holiness to thy Name or Title, & reverence to thy Shadow. Thy Kingship come upon Earth first & then in Heaven. Give us day by day our Real Taxed Substantial Money bought Bread; deliver from the Holy Ghost whatever cannot be Taxed; for all is debts & Taxes between Caesar & us & one another; lead us not to read the Bible, but let our Bible be Virgil & Shakespeare; & deliver us from Poverty in Jesus, that Evil One. For thine is the Kingship, (or) Allegorical Godship, & the Power, or War, & the Glory, or Law, Ages after Ages in thy descendants; for God is only an Allegory of Kings & nothing Else.   Amen."

and finally That God is Colouring Newton does shew,
               And the devil is a Black outline, all of us know.

To Blake, then, the Enemy was the sort of conception of the universe which he associates with Newton, which he regards as having disastrous psychological, religious, political and artistic consequences.

Professor Whitehead has lucidly summarised the essential features of the Newtonian cosmology as follows:

1) The universe consists of ultimate things, whose character is private, with simple location in space.
2) On these is imposed the necessity of entering into relationships with each other. This imposition is the work of God.
3) These imposed behaviour patterns are the laws of Nature.

45

4) You cannot discover the natures so related by any study of the laws.

5) You cannot discover the laws by inspection of the natures.

Associated with this conception there was also that of the Great Chain of Being, i.e., creation was complete, every kind of thing which could possibly exist was already there without room for the admission of any extra novelty, and arranged in an orderly and rationally comprehensible hierarchy of being.

Such a cosmology has important theological consequences. Like the orthodox Christian God and unlike the God of Plato and Aristotle, He is the creator of the world; but unlike the Christian God, and like that of Plato and Aristotle, God and the World have no real mutual relation. While the Greek Universe loves and tries to model itself on the unconscious self-sufficient god, the Newtonian Universe is the passive neutral stuff. God imposes rational order, which it obeys, but to which it does not respond, for the natural world is no longer thought of as an organism.

At first such a concept was not altogether unwelcome to theologians. To an age exhausted by religious wars, weary of unending dogmatic disputes and exasperated by fanatic individual interpretations of Scripture, here at last the possibility of peaceful consent seemed to open up. Here was a god the existence and nature of whom could be ascertained by the use of the human reason which in all sane men comes to the same conclusion, when freed from personal passion and prejudice.

Indeed through the latter half of the seventeenth century and the first half of the eighteenth, there is an attempt in every field, religion, politics, art, etc., to do for that time what their mediaeval predecessors had done for the twelfth and thirteenth centuries, i.e., to construct a new catholic church, catholic society, and catholic art, to found a new Good City on the basis of sound reason, common sense, and good taste.

If the Enlightenment was the precursor of the French Revolution, nothing could have been further from its intentions, which were profoundly conservative and pacifist. The Encyclopaedists did not dream of a new world arising out of the ashes of an old one, but of substituting reason for unreason in the ordering of a human nature and society which was permanently the same at all times. The only necessary change was to substitute for the magic-loving priest or irrational king the rational man of esprit as the leader of the good world society. As Figaro says in Beaumarchais' play:

> Par le sort de la naissance
> L'un est roi, l'autre est berger;
> Le hasard fit leur distance;
> L'esprit seul peut tout changer.
> De vingt rois que l'on encense
> Le trépas brise l'autel
> Et Voltaire est immortel.

The attempt failed, but the history of the preceding two hundred years shows that, insufficient for an ultimate basis as reason, sense and taste turned out to be, they were qualities of which the time stood very much in need.

It is difficult for us to be quite fair to deist theologians like Toland, the author of *Christianity Not Mysterious*, or to hymn-writers like Addison:

> What though in solemn silence, all
> Move round the dark terrestrial ball?
> What though nor real voice nor sound
> Amid their radiant orbs be found?
> In reason's ear they all rejoice,
> And utter forth a glorious voice,
> For ever singing as they shine,
> The hand that made us is divine.

or to the rather cheap sneers of Gibbon or Voltaire, unless we remember the actual horrors of persecution, witch-hunting, and provincial superstition from which they were trying to deliver mankind. Further, the reaction of the Romantics against them is a proof that up to a point they had succeeded. If the final result of their labors was a desert, they had at least drained some very putrid marshes.

However, as Whitehead wittily remarks, such a world view is very easy to understand and extremely difficult to believe.

A transcendent God of Nature of the Newtonian type can be related to the human reason by his intelligibility, and to matter by his power to command exact obedience; the trouble begins when the question is raised of his relation to the human heart, which can and does suffer, and to the human will, which can and does disobey.

Such a Supreme Being could be completely indifferent to human joy or misery, but then he cannot possibly be identified with the Christian God who cares for men and demands their love, worship, and obedience. The attempt so to identify them must result in the purely authoritarian Judge who decrees the moral law and impartially punishes the offender, in fact, the Jehovah, God of This World, whom Blake so detested.

If the moral law is to be completely rational, there can be no contradiction between virtue and practical utility, there cannot be a kingdom of heaven whose values are completely other than the kingdom of this world. In teaching the recalcitrant to resist temptation, it becomes almost inevitable that the reason given will be that virtue succeeds and that vice fails, the Parables offered will be, in fact, the progress of the Virtuous Apprentice who finally marries the master's daughter and the progress of the Rake who ends in Bedlam. Children will be made to pay special attention to such verses as:

> Like some fair tree which, fed by streams
>   With timely fruit doth bend;
> He still shall flourish, and success
>   All his designs attend.
>
> Ungodly men in their attempts
>   No lasting roots shall find

49

> Untimely, withered and dispersed
> Like chaff before the wind.
> (Tate and Brady, Psalm 1.)

With his usual unerring insight Blake saw that the crucial points at issue were the Incarnation of Christ and the Forgiveness of Sins. A Supreme Architect cannot incarnate as an individual, only as the whole building; and a pure Judge cannot forgive; he can only condemn or acquit.

Blake and the other romantics along with him tried in their reaction, not to overcome the dualism, but to stand it on its head,* i.e., to make God purely immanent, so that to Blake God only acts and is in existing beings and men, or is pantheistically diffused through physical nature, not to be perceived by any exercise of the reason, but only through vision and feeling.

---

* More accurately, they absolutise another mode of consciousness. The deist God is an absolutisation of the ego's consciousness of itself as stretching beyond itself, of standing as a spectator apprehending an external reality. The romantic immanent God, on the other hand, is an absolutisation of the ego's consciousness of itself as self-contained, as embracing all of which it is aware in a unity of experiencing. In Hegel, the third mode of consciousness, the ego's consciousness of itself as striving towards is similarly exalted at the expense of the other two modes.

One might say that in deist theology the Son is called the Father and the divinity of the Father is denied, while in romantic theology the divinity of the Son is denied and the Father might more properly be called the Mother.

For a discussion of these heresies in the light of the Catholic teaching of the analogical relation between the Deity and creation see *Polarity* by Erich Przywara (Oxford, 1935), and for the relevance of the Athanasian creed to the artist *The Mind of the Maker* by Dorothy Sayers (Harcourt Brace, 1941).

50

So Coleridge writes:

In the Hebrew poets each thing has a life of its own and yet they are all one life. In God they move and live and *have* their being; not *had*, as the cold system of Newtonian Theology represents, but *have*.

As to the Great Chain of Being, it is retained but in a quite different spirit. The fullness of the universe is felt to be irrational but that is its charm. Thus Schiller writes:

Every kind of perfection must attain existence in the fullness of the world . . . in the infinite chasm of nature no activity could be omitted, no grade of enjoyment be wanting in the universal happiness . . . the Great Inventor could not permit even error to remain unutilized in his great design . . . It is a provision of the supreme wisdom that erring reason should people even the chaotic land of dreams and should cultivate even the barren land of contradiction . . . *Life* and *Liberty* to the greatest possible extent are the glory of the divine creation; nowhere is it more sublime than where it seems to have departed most widely from its ideal.

So too with the problem of evil and suffering. The attempt to explain either in rational terms alone, i.e., as if the question "Why do they exist?" were one primarily raised by the intellect, the substitution for Providence and Wisdom of Economy and Utility, created mysteries more fantastic than any which it replaced, e.g., the suggestion of Soame Jenyns that there might be higher beings who torment us for their pleasure and utility

51

in the same way that we hunt animals, in reply to which
Dr. Johnson composed a famous passage:

"As we drown whelps and kittens, they amuse themselves now
and then with sinking a ship, and stand round the fields of
Blenheim or the walls of Prague, as we encircle a cock-pit. As
we shoot a bird flying, they take a man in the midst of his
business or pleasure, and knock him down with an apoplexy.
Some of them, perhaps, are virtuosi, and delight in the oper-
ations of an asthma, as a human philosopher in the effects of
the air-pump. To swell a man with a tympany is as good sport
as to blow a frog. Many a merry bout have these frolick
beings at the vicissitudes of an ague, and good sport it is to
see a man tumble with an epilepsy, and revive and tumble
again, and all this he knows not why. As they are wiser and
more powerful than we, they have more exquisite diversions,
for we have no way of procuring any sport so brisk and so
lasting, as the paroxysms of the gout and stone, which un-
doubtedly must make high mirth, especially if the play be a
little diversified with the blunders and puzzles of the blind
and deaf."

If such were true, then the only decent human reaction can be that of Captain Ahab, defiance till death.

The Romantic reaction to this is twofold. When they
are objecting to the moralist legalism which thought in
terms of objective infractions of the moral law and its
appropriate penalties, they produce the figure of the
Prelapsarian savage (Queequeg), the innocent sailor
(Budd), or the child of the Immortality Ode, whose
heart is good though he does not consciously understand

or even keep the moral law of the Pharisee. When, on the other hand, they are objecting to the rationalistic optimism which attributes evil to mental ignorance curable by education, they reassert the fallen nature of men and the necessity for conversion.

To the Deists, who thought, like John Sheffield, Duke of Buckingham:

> While in dark Ignorance we lay afraid
> Of Fancies, Ghosts in every empty shade,
> Great Hobbes appeared and by plain Reason's light
> Put such phantastick Forms to shameful Flight.
> Fond is their Fear who think Man needs must be
> To Vice enslaved, if from vain Terrors free:
> The Wise and Good, Morality shall guide
> And Superstition all the World beside.

Blake retorts:

"Man is born a Spectre or Satan and is altogether an Evil, and requires a New Selfhood continually, and must continually be changed into his direct contrary. But your Greek Philosophy (which is a remnant of Druidism) teaches that Man is Righteous in his Vegetated Spectre. . . . Voltaire Rousseau. . . . you are Pharisees and Hypocrites, for you are constantly talking of the Virtues of the Human Heart and particularly of your own, that you may accuse others."

(Jerusalem)

And Baudelaire to the disciples of Voltaire:

"Belief in Progress is a doctrine of idlers and Belgians. . . . True civilisation is not to be found in gas or steam or table-turning. It consists in the diminution of the traces of original sin."

(Mon Coeur Mis à Nu)

POLITICS AND INDIVIDUALISM

Just as it had sought to escape from sectarian fanaticism by establishing a catholic religion of the One Engineer, so the eighteenth century sought to escape from the arbitrariness of absolute monarchy by establishing a catholic society in which all men were equal because they all possessed a body and a mind which obeyed and recognised the same laws. But this over-simplified the nature of man; by denying him an individual soul or by identifying soul with mind, it did indeed make men equal, but with the equality of billiard-balls, not of individual persons. To such a doctrine of a natural law which self-interest guided by common sense will of course accept, the proper answer is that of the hero of Dostoevsky's *Notes from Underground:*

"You will scream at me (that is if you condescend to do so) that no one is touching my free will, that all they are concerned with is that my will should of itself, of its own free will, coincide with my own normal interests, with the laws of nature and arithmetic. Good heavens, gentlemen, what sort of free will is left when we come to tabulation and arithmetic, when it will all be a case of twice two makes four? Twice two makes four without my will. As if free will meant that."

Hence the Romantic reaction stressed the soul and its uniqueness; Herder propounds the uniqueness of the

54

soul of a nation; Schlegel writes: "It is precisely individuality that is the original and eternal theory in men." Novalis declares: "The more personal, local, peculiar, of its own time a poem is, the nearer it stands to the centre of poetry."

Minds may be similar, but they are not the whole or even the chief element in a human being. "I would rather," says Ishmael, "feel your spine than your skull, whoever you are."

The Deist religion of reason had a catholic myth, that of the Goddess of reason, but no cultus, no specifically religious acts; all rational acts were worship of the Goddess.

The romantic reaction replaced the Goddess by a protestant variety of individual myths; but it, too, lacked a cult in which all men could take part. Instead, it substituted imagination for reason, and in place of the man of esprit the artist as the priest-magician.

Art is the tree of life. Art is Christianity.

says Blake.

Poets are the unacknowledged legislators of the world.

says Shelley.

And when Baudelaire says:

There are no great men save the poet, the priest, and the soldier . . . the rest are born for the whip.

(*Mon Coeur Mis à Nu*)

one is not convinced that he cares as much about the last two as about the first.

ROMANTIC AESTHETIC THEORY

Cartesian metaphysics, Newtonian physics and eighteenth-century theories of perception divided the body from the mind, and the primary objects of perception from their secondary qualities, so that physical nature became, as Professor Collingwood says, "matter, infinite in extent, permeated by movement, devoid of ultimate qualitative differences, and moved by uniform and purely quantitative forces," the colorless desert from which Melville recoils:

"All deified nature absolutely paints like a harlot, whose allurements cover nothing but the charnel house within; and when we proceed further, the palsied universe lies before us like a leper."

(Moby Dick. Chapter LXII)

Such a view must naturally affect the theory of artistic composition, for it involves a similar division between the thing to be expressed and the medium in which it is expressed.

"Memory," writes Hobbes, "is the World in which the Judgement, the severer sister, busieth herself in a grave and rigid examination of all the parts of nature and in registering by letters their order, causes, uses, differences, and resemblances; whereby the Fancy, when any work of Art is to be performed, finding her materials at hand and prepared for use, needs no more than a swift motion over them, that what she wants and is there to be had, may not lie too long un-espied."

And Dryden:

"Expression and all that belongs to words is that in a poem which coloring is in a picture . . . Expression is, in plain English, the bawd of her sister, the design . . . she clothes, she dresses her up, she paints her, she makes her appear more lovely than she is."

(Poetry and Painting)

This makes artistic creation an entirely conscious process, and here again we shall not understand its appeal to such great poets as Dryden and Pope unless we understand their wish to escape from chaotic idio-syncrasies, their hope of establishing catholic and objec-tive canons of good taste recognisable by poets and pub-lic alike. Given the subjects with which these poets were passionately concerned—e.g., Dryden was as moved by the play of dialectic as Wordsworth was by Nature, Pope saw in Dulness as great a threat to the City as Dante saw in Sin—the theory did no harm; indeed it did good, for there is a conscious side of creation, and it made the poets take pains at a time when such pains were needed.

A Poem where we all perfections find
Is not the work of a Fantastick mind:

> There must be Care, and Time, and Skill, and Pains;
> Not the first heat of unexperienced brains
> > (Roscommon)

is sound advice.

It was only when poets continued working on the same themes as Dryden and Pope but without their passion, or attempted other kinds of themes to which this diction and treatment were unsuited that the deficiencies of the theory became apparent.

The Romantic reaction, naturally, was to stress imagination and vision; i.e., the less conscious side of artistic creation, the uniqueness of the poet's individual experience, and the symbolic rather than the decorative or descriptive value of images. "What is the modern conception of Art?" asks Baudelaire. "To create a suggestive magic including at the same time object and subject, the world outside the artist and the artist himself." "What is a poet if not a translator, a decipherer?"

THE ROMANTIC USE OF SYMBOLS

To understand the romantic conception of the relation between objective and subjective experience, *Moby Dick* is perhaps the best work to study, partly because in certain aspects it includes preromantic attitudes and treatments which show off the former more clearly than a purely romantic work like *The Ancient Mariner* or *Gordon Pym*.

If we omit the White Whale itself, the whole book is

an elaborate synecdoche, i.e., it takes a particular way of life, that of whale-fishing, which men actually lead to earn their livelihood and of which Melville had first-hand experience and makes it a case of any man's life in general. This literary device is an old one and can be found at all periods; indeed almost all literature does this.

E.g.

1) Whalemen kill for their living. So in one way or another must we all.

2) The proprietors of the *Pequod* are Quakers, i.e., they profess the purest doctrine of non-violence, yet see no incongruity in this; though perhaps Peleg recognises the paradox indirectly when he says: "Pious Harpooners never make good voyages. It takes the shark out of them." So always in every life, except that of the saint or the villain, there is a vast difference between what a man professes and how he acts.

3) The crew are involved in each other's actions and characters. So every world is a world of social relations.

4) In their attitude towards their job of killing whales, they reveal their different characters. Thus Starbuck is a professional who takes no risks unless he has to and will have no man in his boat who is not afraid of the whale. Stubb is a reckless gambler who enjoys risks. Flask follows the fish just for the fun of it. Insofar as the book is this, any other form of activity or

society which Melville happened to know well would have served his purpose.

Then *Moby Dick* is full of parable and typology, i.e., as X is in one field of experience, so is Y in another.

E.g.

"All men live enveloped in whale-lines. All are born with halters round their necks; but it is only when caught in the soft, sudden turn of death that mortals realise the silent subtle ever-present perils of life."

(Chapter LX)

or

"O men, admire—model thyself after the whale. Do thou too remain warm among ice. Do thou, too, live in this world without being of it. Be cool at the Equator, keep thy blood flow at the Pole and retain in all seasons a temperature of thine own."

(Chapter LXVIII)

or again the characters and names of the nine ships (the number is symbol not allegory) which the *Pequod* encounters are, in their relation to Moby Dick, types of the relation of human individuals and societies in the tragic mystery of existence. I.e.,

The *Goney*   The aged who may have experienced the mystery but cannot tell others. (The captain's trumpet falls into the sea.)

The *Town-Ho*	Those who have knowledge of the mystery but keep it secret. (No one tells Ahab the story of Radney and Steelkilt.)
The *Jeroboam*	Those who make a superstitious idolatry of the mystery or whom the mystery has driven crazy.
The *Jungfrau* and the *Rosebud*	Those who out of sloth and avarice respectively will never become aware of the mystery.
The *Enderby*	Those who are aware of the mystery but face it with rational common sense and stoicism. ("What you take for the White Whale's malice is only his awkwardness.")
The *Bachelor*	The frivolous and fortunate who deny the existence of the mystery. ("Have heard of Moby Dick but don't believe in him at all.")
The *Rachel*	Those who have without their understanding or choice become involved in the mystery as the innocents massacred by Herod were involved in the birth of Christ.
The *Delight*	Those whose encounter with the mystery has turned their joy into sorrow.

This analogical method was practised by the Church Fathers in their interpretations of Scripture, and analogies from nature have been common ever since, for example in the Mediaeval Bestiaries or Jonathan Edwards' *Images or Shadows of Divine Things*. It is a conscious process, calling for Judgment and Fancy rather than Imagination, and the one-to-one correspondence asserted is grasped by the reader's reason.

Lastly, in his treatment of the White Whale, Melville uses symbols in the real sense.

A symbol is felt to be such before any possible meaning is consciously recognised; i.e., an object or event which is felt to be more important than the reason can immediately explain is symbolic. Secondly, a symbolic correspondence is never one to one but always multiple, and different persons perceive different meanings. Thus to Ahab "All visible objects, man, are but pasteboard masks. To me the white whale is that wall shoved near to me. Sometimes I think there's naught beyond. I see in him outrageous strength with an insatiable malice sinewing it. That inscrutable thing is chiefly what I hate."

To Gabriel, the mad demagogue who terrorises the *Jeroboam*, its qualities are similar, but his attitude is one of positive idolisation. He worships it as an incarnation of the Shaker God. To Steelkilt of the *Town-Ho* it is the justice and mercy of God, saving him from becoming a murderer and slaying the unjust Radney. To Melville-Ishmael it is neither evil nor good but simply numinous, a declaration of the power and majesty of God which transcends any human standards of ethics. To Starbuck it signifies death or his fatal relation to his captain, the duty which tells him he cannot depart his office to obey, intending open war, yet to have a touch of pity.

THE SHIP AS SYMBOL

If thought of as isolated in the midst of the ocean, a ship can stand for mankind and human society moving through time and struggling with its destiny. If thought of as leaving the land for the ocean, it stands for a particular kind of man and society as contrasted with the average landdwelling kind. *The Hunting of the Snark* is a pure example of the first use, *Twenty Thousand Leagues under the Sea* of the second. In Melville's books, and this is one of the reasons for their fascination, there is a constant interplay between both.

THE SHIP AS MANKIND

A constant aesthetic problem for the writer is how to reconcile his desire to include everything, not to leave anything important out, with his desire for an aesthetic whole, that there shall be no irrelevances and loose ends. The picture has to be both complete and framed. The more society becomes differentiated through division of labor, the more it becomes atomised through urbanisation and through greater ease of communication, the harder it becomes for the artist to find a satisfactory solution.

For, of the traditional wholes, the family becomes representative of one class only, the village the exceptional way of life instead of the typical. The ship is one of the few possible devices left, because, while it is most emphatically a frame—no one can get off or on board once the ship has started—yet it permits of a great deal of variety and interpretation.

E.g.

1) The people on board can show every variety of character as individuals and every age of man from fourteen to seventy. "Wrecked on a desert shore, a man of war's crew could quickly form an Alexandria for themselves."

2) There are a number of social grades: Captain—Mates—Harpooners—Seamen, so that the role of authority in human society and of its dialectical relation to character can be portrayed.

3) A ship has a function to perform, to hunt whales, to fight battles etc., and each member of the crew has his specialised function. The carpenter must carpenter, the boatswain must flog, the chaplain must preach, the master at arms must spy, etc., which allow the exhibition of all the relations between functions, given or chosen, and the character which willingly or unwillingly performs it.

   There can even be passengers without a function.

4) Life on a ship exhibits the distinction and relation between society, i.e., human beings associated for an end, and community, human beings associated

by the tie of a common love or interest. Thus on *The Neversink* there are a number of antagonistic communities within the common society, for instance, the officers versus the common seamen, the rulers whose orders cannot be questioned and the ruled who feel like Melville:

"I was a Roman Jew of the Middle Ages confined to the Jewish quarter of the town and forbidden to stray beyond its limits."

"by far the majority of the common sailors of the *Neversink* were plainly concerned at the prospect of war and were plainly averse to it. But with the officers of the quarterdeck it was just the reverse . . . Because, though war would equally jeopardise the lives of both, yet, while it held out to the sailor no promise of promotion, and what is called *glory*, these things fired the heart of his officers."

(White Jacket)

In the case of the *Pequod*, the situation at the beginning is this: All of the crew with the exception of the captain are a community in that they all want to hunt whales and make money; Ahab stands outside, having no wish to hunt any whale except Moby Dick. He is so far from wishing to make a profitable voyage that, when the barrels begin leaking he would prefer to let them leak rather than delay his quest and only yields to Starbuck's demand to "up Burtons" because he is afraid of mutiny. At the end, however, Ahab has so infected the crew with his passion that they have ceased to care what happens and are made one community with him.

"They were one man, not thirty. For as the one ship that held them all; though it was put together of all contrasting things—oak, and maple, and pine wood; iron, and pitch, and hemp—yet all these ran into each other in the one concrete hull, which shot on its way, both balanced and directed by the long central keel; even so, all the individualities of the crew, this man's valor, that man's fear; guilt and guiltiness, all varieties were welded into oneness, and were all directed to that fatal goal which Ahab their one lord and keel did point to."

(*Moby Dick*. Chapter cxxxiv)

5) As a society which, once you are in (the question of how you get in is only raised when the ship is used in the second symbolic sense of a special kind of life) you cannot get out of, whether you like it or not, whether you approve of it or not, a ship can represent either:

a) The state of being human as decreed by God. Mutiny then is a symbol of the original rebellion of Lucifer and of Adam, the refusal to accept finitude and dependence.

b) The *civitas terrena*, created by self-love, inherited and repeated, into which all men since Adam are born, yet where they have never totally lost their knowledge of and longing for the Civitas Dei and the Law of Love. From this arise absurd contradictions, like the chaplain on a man-of-war who is paid a share of the reward for sinking a ship and cannot condemn war or flogging, or the devout Baptist who earns his bread as captain of a gun.

To be like Christ, to obey the law of love absolutely, is possible only for the saint, for Billy Budd, and even for him the consequence is the same as for Christ, crucifixion. The rest of us cannot avoid disingenuous compliances. Thus, in his dissertation on Chronometricals and Horologicals in *Pierre*, Melville writes:

"Bacon's brains were mere watch-maker's brains; but Christ was a chronometer . . . And the reason why His teachings seemed folly to the Jews, was because he carried that Heaven's time in Jerusalem, while the Jews carried Jerusalem time there . . . as the China watches are right as to China, so the Greenwich chronometers must be wrong as to China. Besides, of what use to the Chinaman would a Greenwich chronometer, keeping Greenwich time, be? Were he thereby to regulate his daily actions, he would be guilty of all manner of absurdities:—going to bed at noon, say, when his neighbors would be sitting down to dinner.*

". . . one thing is to be especially observed. Though Christ encountered woe in both the precept and the practice of His chronometricals, yet did He remain throughout entirely without folly or sin. Whereas, almost invariably, with inferior be-

---

* Cf. the snark

    Its habit of getting up late you'll agree
      That it carries too far when I say
    That it frequently breakfasts at five-o-clock tea
      And dines on the following day.

ings, the absolute effort to live in this world according to the strict letter of the chronometricals is, somehow, apt to involve those inferior beings eventually in strange, *unique* follies and sins, unimagined before."

THE SHIP VERSUS THE CITY

In so far as a ship and its crew sail, whether gladly or sadly, away from the land, where all were born, and leave the majority, whether friends or foes, behind on shore, the mariner image has a different constellation of meanings.

1) *The Search for Possibility and the Escape from Necessity*

Land is the place where people are born, marry, and have children, the world where the changing seasons create a round of different duties and feelings, and the ocean, by contrast, is the place where there are no ties of home or sex, only of duty to the end for which the voyage is undertaken, the world where the change of seasons makes no difference to what the crew must do and where there is no visible life other than theirs, so that to leave land and put out to sea can signify the freeing of the spirit from finite nature, its ascetic denial of the flesh, the determination to live in one-directional historical time rather than in cyclical natural time.

e.g.   *Verse-nous ton poison pour qu'il nous réconforte!*
Nous voulons, tant ce feu nous brûle le cerveau

Plonger au fond du gouffre, Enfer ou Ciel, qu'importe
Au fond de l'Inconnu pour trouver du nouveau.
                                              (*Le Voyage*)

i.e. the flight from finite repetition to infinite novelty.

Plus douce qu'aux enfants la chair des pommes sures,
L'eau verte pénétra ma coque de sapin
Et des taches de vins bleus et des vomissures
Me lava, dispersant gouvernail et grappin.
                                              (*Bâteau Ivre*)

Pour n'être pas changés en bêtes, ils s'enivrent
D'espace et de lumière et de cieux embrasés;
La glace qui les mord, les soleils qui les cuivrent,
Effacent lentement la marque des baisers.
                                              (*Le Voyage*)

i.e., the purification from debauchery and sex. "The *Nautilus* is a place of refuge for those who, like its commander, have broken every tie upon earth."

i.e., the flight from injustice.

". . . Come hither, broken-hearted; here is another life without the guilt of intermediate death; here are wonders supernatural, without dying for them. Come hither! bury thyself in a life which, to your now equally abhorred and abhorring, landed world, is more oblivious than death. Come hither! put up thy grave-stone, too, within the churchyard, and come hither, till we marry thee!"

Hearkening to these voices, East and West, by early sun-

69

rise, and by fall of eve, the blacksmith's soul responded, Aye, I come! And so Perth went a-whaling.

(Moby Dick. Chap. cxii)

i.e., the flight from memory.

Away O soul! hoist instantly the anchor!
Cut the hawsers—haul out—shake out every sail!
Have we not stood here like trees in the ground long enough?
Have we not grovel'd here long enough, eating and drinking
like mere brutes?
Have we not darken'd and dazed ourselves with books long
enough?

Sail forth—steer for the deep waters only,
Reckless O soul, exploring, I with thee, and thou with me.
For we are bound where mariner has not yet dared to go.
And we will risk the ship, ourselves and all.

(Passage to India)

i.e., the rejection of conventional habit.

2) *The Search for Necessity and the Escape from Possibility*

The fact that a ship is a strictly disciplined and authoritarian society as compared with normal life, and that a ship has a purpose for a voyage, means that ship and city can have almost exactly the opposite significance to the above, i.e., the land can be thought of as the

noir océan de l'immonde cité,

the place of purposelessness, of the ennui that comes

from being confronted with infinite possibilities without the necessity to choose one.

So, for instance, in Ishmael's case, or in Melville's enlistment on the *Neversink*, their going to sea is a commitment to a necessity which, however unpleasant, is at least certain and preferable to the melancholia and accidie induced by the meaningless freedom on shore.

THE ENVIRONMENT OF THE SHIP

The ship, i.e., the human, individual or social, is related to two pairs of contrasting symbols, i.e.,

A. The sky and its creatures, birds
vs.
The water and its creatures, fish, whales, octopuses, etc.

B. The day and the sun and to two scales of weather.
vs.
The night and the moon .

The degree of visibility.
From very clear to thick fog.

The velocity of the wind.
From typhoon to dead calm.

The symbolism is easier to grasp in the purely imaginary voyages like those of Coleridge, Baudelaire and Rimbaud than in the work of Melville and Hopkins, where there is the extra complication of the relation of objective reality to subjective meaning.

A

Sky as contrasted with water = Spirit as contrasted with Nature.

What comes from the sky is a spiritual or supernatural visitation.

What lies hidden in the water is the unknown powers of nature.

E.g.

Cp. the angelic spirits sent by the Moon, or Master of the sea, who move the Ancient Mariner's ship by removing the air in front of it, and the avenging spirit from the land of ice and snow which dwells nine fathoms below the surface and at their command unwillingly moves the ship up to the line.

Cp. The Albatross which is related to the Dove of the Holy Spirit, and through him to the innocent victim, Christ, the water-snakes which are that in nature, whether outside man or within himself, for which he feels aversion because he cannot understand them aesthetically or intellectually and despises because he cannot make use of them. But for the Fall (the shooting of the Albatross), Adam (The Ancient Mariner) would never have consciously learned through suffering the meaning of Agapé, i.e., to love one's neighbour as oneself without comparisons or greed (the blessing of the snakes), so that the Ancient Mariner might well say in the end, *O felix culpa.*

Similarly the hawk in *Moby Dick* is the messenger bird of Zeus who warns Prometheus-Ahab of his hybris when he cheats the lookout by snatching away his hat, i.e., his heroic crown, but whom in its last death-defiance the *Pequod* drags down with it. Contrasted with him is the great squid, messenger of the underworld, whose appearance frightens Starbuck more than the whale itself.

In *Un Voyage à Cythère*, the doves of Venus have been metamorphosed into ferocious crows who devour the male corpse.

B

Day and the Sun = Consciousness and the Paternal
        Principle as contrasted with

Night and the Moon = Unconsciousness and the
        Maternal Principle.

In his excellent essay on *The Ancient Mariner*,[*] Mr. Robert Penn Warren has pointed out how all the events of salvation take place under the influence of the moon, and that the sun is the hostile judge of conscience.

The Father Sun can appear at night in the form of lightning.

E.g.

> The thick black cloud was cleft, and still
> The Moon was at its side:

---

[*] The Rime of The Ancient Mariner. (Reynal & Hitchcock, 1946)

> Like waters shot from some high crag,
> The lightning fell with never a jag,
> A river steep and wide.

Here the Ancient Mariner, so afraid of the Father, is comforted by knowing that the Mother is still present. Again when Captain Ahab addresses the lightning, on a night without a moon, he says:

"Thou art my fiery father; my sweet mother I know not. What hast thou done with her?"

And Hopkins, addressing God:

> I did say yes
> O at lightning and lashed rod;
> Thou heardst me truer than tongue confess
> Thy terror, O Christ, O God;
> Thou knowest the walls, altar and hour and night:
> The swoon of a heart that the sweep and the hurl of thee
> trod
> Hard down with a horror of height:
> And the midriff astrain with leaning of, laced with fire of stress.

VISIBILITY

The degree of visibility = the degree of conscious knowledge.
I.e., fog and mist mean doubt and self-delusion, a clear day knowing where one is going or exactly what one has done.

74

THE WIND

The wind is always a force which the conscious will cannot cause or control. In the works we are considering which were written before the advent of the steamship, it is also the source, good or bad, of all the movements of life.

In *The Ancient Mariner* there are four winds described.

1) The tyrannous strong wind which chases the ship down to the dangerous land of icebergs, mist and snow, against her will.

> With sloping masts and dipping prow,
> As who pursued with yell and blow
> Still treads the shadow of his foe,
> And forward bends his head,
> The ship drove fast, loud roared the blast,
> And southward aye we fled.

Man, that is, is driven on by an irresistible rush of creative powers which he did not expect and which frighten him because he does not know where they are carrying him except that it is probably into a state of dread. The powers, however, are not necessarily evil. They only, as it turns out, drive him into temptation, for the icebergs represent that state of dread which Kierkegaard describes as the necessary precondition for the Fall.

Dread is a desire for what one fears, a sympathetic antipathy; dread is an alien power which takes hold of the individual,

75

and yet one cannot extricate oneself from it, does not wish to, because one is afraid, but what one fears attracts one. Dread renders the individual powerless, and the first sin always happens in a moment of weakness; it therefore lacks any accountableness, but that want is the real snare.*

(*The Concept of Dread*)

2) The good south wind which extricates them from the ice. This is not frightening because it takes the ego where the ego thinks it wants to go. In fact, it turns out to be, like the first elation of Adam and Eve after eating the apple, a delusion, for it disappears and leaves them in the absolute calm of guilt and despair, bereft of all power.

3) The roaring wind which is only heard and never touches the Mariner or the ship, but brings rain, and at the sound of which angelic spirits occupy the bodies of the dead crew. To hear and not feel, means to intuit the possibility and hope for the coming of the new life which one still does not know as an actuality.

4) Finally, when his repentance is complete, so that he can even look away from the dead men (the proof of his sin), then comes the gentle wind which fans his cheek and leads the ship back home, i.e., the powers of grace and blessing.

In *Bateau Ivre*, the wind is usually violent and inevi-

---

* *The Voyage of Maeldune* begins with a similar violent wind which does just the opposite; it takes the hero intent on vengeance away from opportunity to become guilty.

table, but the point is that the hero of the poem deliberately surrenders to it. He enjoys defiantly its irrationality and disorder, and speaks of

> *tohus-bohus . . . triomphants*
> *La tempête a béni mes éveils maritimes.*
>
> *J'ai suivi, des mois pleins, pareille aux vacheries*
> *Hystériques, la houle à l'assaut des récifs,*
> *Sans songer que les pieds lumineux des Maries*
> *Pussent forcer le mufle aux Océans poussifs.*
>
> *Des écumes de fleurs ont béni mes dérades*
> *Et d'ineffables vents m'ont ailé par instants.*

The final result, however, is exhaustion, the state of all-too-real calm, and lack of relation.

> *Mais, vrai, j'ai trop pleuré. Les aubes sont navrantes,*
> *Toute lune est atroce et tout soleil amer . . .*
>
> *Je ne puis plus, baigné de vos langueurs, ô lames,*
> *Enlever leur sillage aux porteurs de cotons.*
>
> *(Bateau Ivre)*

In *Moby Dick*, where the weather is real weather in nature, the point is the relation of human nature to non-human nature, i.e., the kind of importance that the human characters attribute to it. E.g., the typhoon is significant to two of the characters, Starbuck and Ahab.

"Here!" cried Starbuck, seizing Stubb by the shoulder, and pointing his hand towards the weather bow, "markest thou not that the gale comes from the eastward, the very course

77

Ahab is to run for Moby Dick? . . . The gale that now hammers at us to stave us, we can turn it into a fair wind that will drive us towards home."

(Chapter CXIX)

His disapproval of Ahab's quest is strengthened by this omen to the point where he goes down to Ahab's cabin with the intention of killing him as a madman. Ahab, on the other hand, is tempted precisely because the Typhoon is in opposition to the way he has sworn to go.

"I own thy speechless, placeless power; but to the last gasp of my earthquake life will dispute its unconditional unintegral mastery in me . . . Come in thy lowest form of love, and I will kneel and kiss thee; but at thy highest, come as mere supernal power; and though thou launchest navies of full-freighted worlds, there's that in here that still remains indifferent."

(Chapter CXIX)

A calm, such as the beautiful day, before the final chase begins, which offers no outside opposition, makes him think of wife and child, and nearly wins him over to Starbuck's side and to giving up the quest.

The use of the tempest in *The Wreck of the Deutschland* is still more complicated.

We have the physical contrasted situation of Hopkins, the Jesuit novice

> Away in the loveable west,
> On a pastoral forehead of Wales,
> I was under a roof here, I was at rest,

and of the nuns

> And they the prey of the gales

and in counterpoint to this is the subjective contrast of their inner peace in the face of death:

> Ah! there was a heart right!
> There was single eye!
> Read the unshapeable shock night
> And knew the who and the why;
> Wording it how but by him that present and past,
> Heaven and earth are word of, worded by?
> The Simon Peter of a soul! to the blast
> Tarpeian-fast, but a blown beacon of light

with his inner tempest in his struggle to submit his self-will to the will of God, on the necessity of which St. Ignatius lays so much importance.

> The frown of his face
> Before me, the hurtle of hell
> Behind, where, where was a, where was a place?

Both kinds of tempest are related as forms of suffering, but also carefully differentiated. The suffering that arises out of the relation of the soul to God only arises because of the human sin of which the climax was the Crucifixion:

> The dense and the driven Passion, and frightful sweat;
> Thence the discharge of it, there its swelling to be,
> Though felt before, though in high flood yet—

79

What none would have known of it, only the heart, being hard
    at bay

The relation was intended to be one of joy, and the intensity of the struggle is a direct indication of the amount
of self-will to be overcome, i.e., spiritual suffering is to
be treated as purgatorial, i.e., the sufferer must embrace it, saying, "I say pain but ought to say solace."

External suffering, on the other hand, is something
different. No one who is shipwrecked or diseased is to be
considered as more or less sinful than fortunate people.
Nevertheless, nature is the handiwork of God.

They fought with God's cold.

All that the individual can do is accept it as he or she
must accept every other event pleasant or unpleasant
that happens to him, as a challenge, not to despair like
Starbuck, not to defy like Ahab, but as an occasion to
ask what in this actual situation sent by God God requires.

In this case the nuns who are innocent exiles

Loathed for a love men knew in them,
Banned by the land of their birth,
Rhine refused them. Thames would ruin them.

by their conduct in this disaster are a witness to their
faith which in the very moment of physical destruction
may have saved some souls from spiritual death.

Well, she has thee for the pain, for the
Patience; but pity of the rest of them!

Heart, go and bleed at a bitterer vain for the
        Comfortless unconfessed of them—
No not uncomforted: lovely-felicitous Providence
Finger of a tender of, O of a feathery delicacy, the breast
        of the
        Maiden could obey so, be a bell to, ring of it, and
Startle the poor sheep back! is the shipwrack then a harvest,
    does tempest carry the grain for thee?

THE STONE, THE ROMANTICS AND
MATHEMATICS

Whereas the Neoclassical writers had been taught to observe particular natural objects carefully and accurately and then abstract the general from them, the Romantics reverse the process. Thus Blake says: "All goodness resides in minute particulars" but "Natural objects always did and now do weaken, deaden and obliterate imagination in me" and Coleridge writes in a letter:

"The further I ascend from animated Nature (i.e., in the embracements of rocks and hills), from men and cattle, and the common birds of the woods and fields, the greater becomes in me the intensity of the feeling of life. Life seems to me then a universal spirit that neither has nor can have an opposite."

As long as images derived from observation of nature had a utility value for decorating the thoughts of the mind, nature could be simply enjoyed, for Nature was

81

not very important by comparison with human reason. But if there is a mysterious relation between them, if

> *La Nature est un temple où de vivants piliers*
> *Laissent parfois sortir de confuses paroles;*
> *L'homme y passe à travers des forêts de symboles*
> *Qui l'observent avec des regards familiers.*
>
> *Comme de longs échos qui de loin se confondent*
> *Dans une ténébreuse et profonde unité,*
> *Vaste comme la nuit et comme la clarté,*
> *Les parfums, les couleurs et les sons se répondent,*
> Baudelaire (Correspondances)

then the merely visual perception is not the important act, but the intuitive vision of the meaning of the object, and also Nature becomes a much more formidable creature, charged with all the joys, griefs, hopes and terrors of the human soul, and therefore arousing very mixed feelings of love and hatred.

On the one hand, the poets long to immerse in the sea of Nature, to enjoy its endless mystery and novelty, on the other, they long to come to port in some transcendent eternal and unchanging reality from which the unexpected is excluded. Nature and Passion are powerful, but they are also full of grief. True happiness would have the calm and order of bourgeois routine without its utilitarian ignobility and boredom.

Thus the same Baudelaire who writes:

"Why is the spectacle of the sea so infinitely and eternally agreeable?

"Because the sea presents at once the idea of immensity

and of movement . . . Twelve or fourteen leagues of liquid in movement are enough to convey to man the highest expression of beauty which he can encounter in his transient abode."

(Mon Coeur Mis à Nu)

and identifies human nature with the sea:

> *Vous êtes tous les deux ténébreux et discrets*
> *Homme, nul n'a sondé le fond de tes abîmes,*
> *O mer, nul ne connaît tes richesses intimes*
> *Tant vous êtes jaloux de garder vos secrets!*
> (L'Homme et la Mer)

also exclaims:

> *Ah! ne jamais sortir des Nombres et des Êtres*

and likens Beauty to a dream of stone (cp. the stone of Wordsworth's dream):

> *Je hais le mouvement qui déplace les lignes,*
> *Et jamais je ne pleure et jamais je ne ris.*

And the amorous Henry Beyle who cannot live without a grand passion writes:

"I used to imagine that the higher mathematics dealt with all, or almost all, aspects of things, and that, by proceeding to their study, I should arrive at a knowledge of all things that were certain, irrefutable, and demonstrable at will. I said to myself, 'mathematics will get me out of Grenoble, out of that sickening morass.' "

So too in *The Hunting of the Snark* the Beaver and the Butcher, romantic explorers though they are, who have chosen to enter a desolate valley, where the Jub-Jub bird screams in passion overhead, and the creatures from *The Temptation of St. Anthony* surround them, escape from the destructive power of sex sublimating it into arithmetical calculations based on the number 3.

And Melville, despite his love of physical beauty, in nature and in man, of

> our Pantheistic ports:
> Marquesas and glenned isles that be
> Authentic Edens in a Pagan sea.

can also note in revulsion:

> Found a family, build a state,
> The pledged event is still the same:
> Matter in end will never abate
> His ancient brutal claim.

Baudelaire's ideal man, the Dandy, is, from the point of view of the bourgeois, a wild figure who indulges in every kind of excess, but, from his own, he is a fastidious ascetic who despises the bourgeois because they are "natural."

"Woman is the opposite of the Dandy. Therefore she should inspire horror. Woman is hungry and she wants to eat, thirsty and she wants to drink. She is in rut and she wants to be possessed. Woman is *natural*, that is to say, abominable.

"The Dandy should aspire to be uninterruptedly sublime. He should live and sleep in front of a mirror.

"The more a man cultivates the arts, the less he fornicates.

84

A more and more apparent cleavage occurs between the spirit
and the brute."

(Mon Cœur Mis à Nu)

The Euclidean stone, the transcendent stable reality
desired as a haven for the storm-tossed mariner, is not,
however, the Transcendental Newtonian God but
rather the Platonic Ideas. Geometry does not judge or
interfere but is beyond good and evil; it demands nothing but what the mind cares to give it; moreover, it
cannot be made use of, it is not one of those ignoble
social snarks, you cannot fetch it home and serve it with
greens: it is not for striking a light, it is simply itself,
and to be oneself is the aim of every romantic.

When Peer Gynt visits the land of the Trolls, the
king puts him through a catechism:

K. What is the difference between Trolls and Men?
P. There isn't any, as far as I can gather;
    Big trolls would roast and little ones would claw you—
    Just as with us if only we dared do it.
K. True; we're alike in that and other things too.
    Still, just as morning's different from evening,
    So there's a real difference between us,
    And I will tell you what it is. Out yonder
    Under the skies men have a common saying:
    "Man, to thyself be true!" But here, 'mongst Trolls
    "Troll, to thyself be—enough."

(Peer Gynt ii. 6)

To be enough to oneself means to have no conscious ego
standing over against the self, to be unable to say no to

85

oneself, or to distinguish fantasy from reality, not to
be able to lie, to have no name and answer to Hi or to
any loud cry. The siren voice of the poetic shell calls
men to the sea, the double kingdom, to put off their
human nature and be Trolls. The prospect is as alluring
to every man as it was to Faust:

> *Hier fass ich Fuss! Hier sind es Wirklichkeiten,*
> *Von hier aus darf der Geist mit Geistern streiten,*
> *Das Doppelreich, das grosse, sich bereiten.*
> *So fern sie war, wie kann sie näher sein!*
> *Ich rette sie und sie ist doppelt mein.*
>
> (*Faust.* Part II. 1. 5)

yet every man makes his reservations like Peer Gynt.

> I've taken a tail, it is true; but then
> I can undo the knots that our friend has tied,
> And take the thing off. I have shed my breeches;
> They were old and patched; but that won't prevent me
> From putting them on if I have a mind to.
> I shall probably find it just as easy
> To deal with your Trollish way of living.
> I can easily swear that a cow's a maiden;
> An oath's not a difficult thing to swallow.
> But to know that one never can get one's freedom—
> Not even to die as a human being—
> To end one's day as a Troll of the mountains—
> Never go back, as you tell me plainly—
> That is a thing that I'll not submit to.
>
> (*Peer Gynt* II. 6)

For to submit would be to be swallowed up in the waters, to be drowned in the deluge.

On the other side, the Euclidean stone speaks of a world of pure truth, the image to the weary mariner of all that is true to itself. It is, however, not truth which is enough to itself, and no man can be as a triangle any more than he can be as a troll, for he would have to lose his self and become a purely self-conscious ego whose motto would be "I to I be enough." This is the dilemma of the romantic hero.

THREE

Ishmael—Don Quixote

wwwwww

"Mes soeurs, n'aimez pas les marins:
La solitude est leur royaume."

JEAN COCTEAU

WHAT IS A HERO? THE EXCEPTIONAL INDIVIDUAL. HOW is he recognised, whether in life or in books? By the degree of interest he arouses in the spectator or the reader. A comparative study, therefore, of the kinds of individuals which writers in various periods have chosen for their heroes often provides a useful clue to the attitudes and preoccupations of each age, for a man's interest always centres, consciously or unconsciously, round what seems to him the most important and still unsolved problem. The hero and his story are simultaneously a stating and a solving of the problem.

HEROIC AUTHORITY

The exceptional individual is one who possesses authority over the average. This authority can be of three kinds, aesthetic, ethical and religious.

AESTHETIC AUTHORITY

Aesthetic authority arises from a necessary inequality of finite individuals in relation to one another. The aesthetic hero is the man to whom fortune has granted exceptional gifts. These may be within himself, e.g., A is more beautiful or cleverer than B, or in the situation in which he is placed, e.g., A is a king, B is a slave.

The inequality is necessary in the first case because beauty or brains are given qualities which cannot be produced or exchanged by any voluntary decision on either side, and in the second because, at any given moment of time in the situation, authority is given to the one.

Since, by virtue of his superior gifts, the hero can do what the average cannot do for themselves, he must do precisely that to be recognised by them as a hero. Thus, if victory over their enemies is what they most desire, he must lead them in war; if victory over nature, he must construct bridges, drain swamps, etc. In return they must give him admiration and obedience. The natural threat to the aesthetic hero is the passing of time, culminating in the inevitable fact of death, which brings him to the same level of nullity as everyone else.

There are also dangers within himself and within the others. For him the danger is pride, i.e., thinking that his superior qualities are not given him by the gods or fate or nature, but earned by him, i.e., that he is not merely luckier than others but intrinsically morally better. If he yields to this, he becomes a tyrant who demands admiration in excess and is insolent towards the powers that gave him his power. Vice versa, the danger for the average is envy, i.e., denying that the inequality is necessary, and wishing to take the hero's place or, if that is impossible, at least to bring him down to their level.

The aesthetic hero is naturally thought of as being happy, for all desire to be as he. He only becomes unhappy when he ceases to be superior, i.e., when he dies, or suffers some great misfortune.

The Homeric kind of hero is pathetic, i.e., his death happens to him without any fault on his part. The hero of Greek drama is tragic because his death is due to pride on his part, and envy on the part of the gods.

ETHICAL AUTHORITY

Ethical authority arises from an accidental inequality in the relation of individuals to the universal truth. The ethical hero is the one who at any given moment happens to know more than the others. This knowledge can be any part of the truth, not only what is commonly called ethics.

E.g. A is ethically superior in relation to B if he knows the multiplication table up to 11 when B only knows it up to 10, just as C is to D, if C knows that it is wrong to steal and D does not yet know it.

Here it is not a question of innate gifts (if A is cleverer than B he is aesthetically superior) but a remediable accident of time and opportunity, i.e., the hero is not one who *can* do what the others cannot, but one who *does* know now what the others *do* not but can be taught by him, which is precisely what he must do if he is to be recognised by them as a hero. In return they give him their attention, as a bridge between them and the truth, for what is required of both is exactly the same, to love and to learn as much about the truth as possible. It is quite possible, for instance, that if A teaches B the eleven times table, so making them equal, B now learns the twelves table before A, and their positions are reversed. It is now B who is the hero.

Here again there are dangers both from without and within. "Without," however, now has a special sense, it means outside the mind, i.e., not from time or fate, but from matter, the needs and passions of the body which interfere with love and study of the truth.

The inner danger is the same for both hero-teacher and inferior pupil, namely, that they will both attempt to treat the situation as an aesthetic relation between them and forget or deny their relations to the truth, which is the important thing. Thus the ethical hero, desiring aesthetic admiration, is tempted to refuse to surrender his superiority and refuse to share his knowledge, treating it instead as a hermetic mystery, the consequence of which is that, thinking always of his relation to the ignorant, he ceases to think about the truth. The inferior, desiring ease and bodily pleasure, are tempted either to refuse to learn from the hero or to adopt a passive attitude of admiration which takes what he says because he says, and not because they can see for themselves that it is the truth.

The Ethical Hero, e.g., Socrates, is thought of as one who is happier than his inferiors because he is already in the movement away from the dark misery of ignorance and servitude to passion towards the bright joy of freedom in knowledge of the truth. Time is not the ultimately overwhelming enemy, but the temporary element through which men move towards immortality.

RELIGIOUS AUTHORITY

Religious authority is like aesthetic authority in that it is not transferable from one individual to another and like ethical authority in that it arises, not from a relation between individuals, but from a relation to truth. But the religious definition of truth is not that it is universal but that it is absolute. The religious hero is one who is committed to anything with absolute passion, i.e., to him it is the absolute truth, his god. The stress is so strongly on the absolute that though he may be passionately related to what, ethically, i.e., universally, is false, he is a religious hero and has religious authority over the one who is lukewarmly or dispassionately related to what is true. Thus, the distinction between being absolutely committed to the real truth, and being absolutely committed to falsehood, is not between being a religious man or not being one, but between the sane and the mad.

In a sense, the religious hero is not related to others at all: his authority cannot command admiration, or transfer knowledge, it can only enkindle by example a similar absolute passion, not necessarily for the same god. (E.g., one has sometimes observed in education that a teacher with a passion for, say, mathematics, has aroused in an unmathematical pupil a passion for, say, Latin.)

The dangers for the religious hero are two: firstly, that he may lose his faith, and so cease to be absolutely committed, and secondly and much more seriously that while continuing to recognise the absolute commitment he should transmute its nature from positive to negative, so that he is committed to the truth in an absolute passion of aversion and hatred. In the first case, he simply ceases to be a religious hero; in the second, he becomes the negative religious hero, i.e., the devil, the absolute villain, Iago or Claggart. The temptation to either arises from expecting something in return for his commitment, i.e., the aesthetic hero may expect happiness so long as he possesses his gifts, but it is his happiness that is a temptation to pride, the ethical hero can look forward to more and more true happiness so long as he perseveres, but it is the pleasures of the body that tempt him to give up his quest, but the religious hero cannot demand happiness, except the happiness of the commitment itself, of love for love's sake. It does not follow that he must necessarily expect misery though, since few desire misery, it is usually misery and not happiness or pleasure that are his temptation; it is more correct to say that whatever he does not expect is temptation.

THE ROMANTIC HERO

In Wordsworth's dream, the hero is described as a combination of a Bedouin desert dweller and Don Quixote; his intention is to carry away symbols of imagination and abstract reason to hide them from the destructive deluge to come; his motive, to save them for future descendants of men, for the age after the Flood. His end is left in doubt, but it seems probable that it is tragic, that he is overwhelmed and fails to save the treasures entrusted to him. Why a Bedouin and why Don Quixote?

ISHMAEL

The Biblical story of the first Bedouin, Ishmael, is given in *Genesis* (chapters XVI and XVII, and chapter XXI). Abraham's wife Sarah is barren, so at her suggestion Abraham lies with a bond-maiden, Hagar. Sarah now becomes jealous and with Abraham's consent treats the pregnant Hagar so badly that she runs away into the desert. But there an angel speaks to her and tells her to return to her mistress, and prophesies:

Behold, thou shalt bear a son, and shalt call his name Ishmael. He will be a wild man; his hand will be against every man, and every man's hand against him: and he shall dwell in the midst of all his brethren.

God also speaks to Abraham:

Sarah thy wife shall bear thee a son indeed and thou shalt call his name Isaac . . . As for Ishmael . . . Behold, I have

96

blessed him, and will make him a great nation. But my cove-
nant shall be with Isaac which Sarah shall bear unto thee at
this set time in the next year.

In due order first Ishmael and then Isaac are born, but
Sarah is still jealous—in fairness to her she has both
before and now caught Hagar mocking at her—and says
to Abraham:

"Cast out this bondwoman and her son; for the son of this
bondwoman shall not be heir with my son, even with Isaac."
And the thing was very grievous in Abraham's sight because
of his son. And God said unto Abraham, Let it not be grievous
in thy sight because of the lad, and because of thy bondwoman; in all that Sarah hath said unto thee, hearken unto
her voice; for in Isaac shall thy seed be called.
And also of the son of the bondwoman will I make a nation,
because he is thy seed.

Abraham accordingly gives Hagar and Ishmael some
bread and water and turns them out into the desert
where they are about to die of thirst, when God shows
her a well and tells her too that he will make a great
nation of Ishmael.

And God was with the lad; and he grew, and dwelt in the
wilderness, and became an archer.

Translating this story into terms of personality, we get
someone who
1) Is conscious of superior powers. (The first-born)
2) Has a grievance, feeling that he is the victim of some
   wrong for which he is not responsible. (Illegitimate)

3) Does not like and is not liked by the respectable, fashionable and successful of this world (Sarah and Isaac). He despises them for not being gifted as he (Hagar's mocking of Sarah) and they envy and persecute him for the same reason. (Sarah's behaviour towards Hagar)

4) In consequence he is socially an outcast and not easily employable. If he does fall in love, it is an unhappy love. (He dwells in the wilderness)

5) He prefers to spend his time with other social outcasts like himself, with crooks, whores, impressed sailors, etc., of whom there are a good many. (A great nation)

6) In solitude and low company he develops the qualities of courage and tough endurance. (An archer)

7) He is unhappy and lonely, yet cherishes his unhappiness and loneliness as a proof of his superiority. (He chooses to live in the desert)

DON QUIXOTE

When we are first introduced to Don Quixote he is
1) poor
2) not a knight but only the plain Alonso Quixano
3) has had a sort of inclination for a good country lass, though 'tis believed she never heard of it
4) has nothing to do except hunt and read romances about Knight Errantry
5) is slightly mad, i.e., he sells land to buy these books.

Suddenly he goes really mad: i.e., instead of being content to project himself in imagination into the heroes of the books, he sets out to become in reality what he admires and rides off to restore to the fallen world the golden age of chivalry, and to challenge all comers to admit that the obscure country girl is the Princess Dulcinea del Toboso, the most beautiful woman in the world. Naturally enough, he fails in everything. When he thinks he is attacking giants, heretics and heathens he is not only worsted in combat, but attacks innocent people and destroys other people's property.

Further, his madness has two aspects: firstly, the nature of his resolution and secondly the moments in which he sees people and objects as other than they are. The first is constant, the second intermittent. Yet when his vision is sane, i.e., when he sees that the windmills are windmills and not giants, it does not change his original conviction, for he takes his moments of sane vision to be mad and says, "These cursed magicians delude me, first drawing me into dangerous adventures by the appearances of things as they really are and then presently changing the face of things as they please." Even when they meet a plain country wench, whom Don Quixote correctly sees as such, and Sancho Panza for a joke describes her as his ideal lady, the Princess Dulcinea, he believes Sancho Panza against the evidence of his own feelings.

Finally, after many adventures, all of them unsuccessful, he falls sick, and suddenly he recovers his sanity. His friends wish him to go on being mad and to provide them with fresh amusement, but he says simply: "Ne'er look for birds of this year in the nests of the last: I was mad and am now in my senses: I was once Don Quixote de la Mancha but am now the plain Alonso Quixano, and I hope the sincerity of my words and my repentance may restore me the same esteem you have had for me before." Whereupon he dies.

Don Quixote is, of course, a representation, the greatest in literature, of the Religious Hero, whose faith is never shaken and whose characteristics we have already discussed. The only point to consider here is why Cervantes makes him recover his sanity at the end. Does this mean that he ceases to be a religious hero, that he loses his faith? No. It is because Cervantes realises instinctively that the Religious Hero cannot be accurately portrayed in art. Art is bound by its nature to make the hero interesting, i.e., to be recognisable as a hero by others. Both the aesthetic hero and the ethical hero are necessarily interesting and recognisable by their deeds and their knowledge, but it is accidental and irrelevant if the religious hero is so recognised or not. Unless Don Quixote recovers his senses, it would imply that the Religious Hero is always also an aesthetic hero (which is what his friends want him to be). On the other hand, once he does, he has to die, for he becomes uninteresting and therefore cannot live in a book.

ISHMAEL AND DON QUIXOTE
COMPARED

1) Both are solitaries, despised and rejected by the world. But while Ishmael retreats from society, Don Quixote seeks a relation with it and it is just this attempt that gets him into trouble. As long as he stayed in his library alone reading, he was free from misfortune.

2) Both are unhappy. But while Ishmael has a grievance and is sorry for himself, Don Quixote is only unhappy because he is sorry the world is not the world which for its own sake it should be; he is not sorry for himself but ashamed of himself for being unable to cure the world of its sickness.

3) Both are unsuccessful in love; but while Ishmael is sorry because his love is not returned, Don Quixote never thinks of reciprocation and is only ashamed because he cannot prove his love.

4) Both consort with and enjoy low company; but while Ishmael enjoys it because it is low and vicious, Don Quixote enjoys it because he is persuaded that it is noble and virtuous.

5) Both are brave and tough; but while Ishmael congratulates himself on this fact, Don Quixote takes it for granted without thinking.

6) Both are wanderers; but while Ishmael is a wanderer because he lacks a definite commitment to any person or goal, it is just his mania of commitment which turns the peaceful stay-at-home Alonso Quixano

101

into the pugnacious vagabond Don Quixote de la Mancha.

7) Ishmael has gifts which he will not put at the service of others, i.e., he does not try to be recognised as the aesthetic or ethical hero which he is.

Don Quixote, on the other hand, has no gifts yet tries desperately to be of use. He is not an aesthetic or ethical hero but goes on trying, in the face of constant failure, to become one.

The crucial difference between them, in fact, is that Ishmael is self-conscious and Don Quixote is completely self-forgetful.

THE HEROIC ACTION

The heroes of Classical and Renaissance literature (with the exception of Hamlet) are recognisable as heroic through the nature of their relations to other men, i.e., of their social acts. The hero is the one who conquers and rules others, or who teaches others. If he suffers a tragic fall, it is a social fall, he is overthrown by a stronger hero, or commits crimes which arouse public horror, or, like Socrates, is executed for being a political danger.

But our dream Ishmael–Don Quixote is quite alone. He is plainly not a conqueror. He is related to knowledge, i.e., he is the sole guardian of the imagination and the reason, the two human forms of knowledge, but he does not teach anyone else; he keeps the shell and the stone to himself. He is apparently performing a social act; he is trying to save these treasures for the sake of the future world, but there is no one around to recognise what he is doing, and even the I of the dreamer loses sight of him and does not know his end, whether or not he succeeded.

Taking such a figure as an archetype, we may now consider the romantic writers, their critical statements and the heroes of their books, and ask: What role does Ishmael play in their work? What role does Don Quixote play? How are these two related? What is the romantic hero up to?

1) There is almost universal agreement that one of the distinguishing marks of the hero is that he is always unhappy. To be happy is almost a proof that one is not a hero. For instance:

I have found a definition of the Beautiful, of my own conception of the Beautiful. It is something intense and sad, leaving scope for conjecture . . . A beautiful male head . . . will suggest ardours and passions—spiritual longings—ambitions darkly repressed—powers turned to bitterness through lack of employment—traces, sometimes, of a revengeful coldness (for the archetype of the dandy must not be forgotten here), sometimes, also—and this is one of the most interesting characteristics of Beauty—of mystery, and last of all (let me admit the exact point to which I am a modern in my aesthetics) of Unhappiness. I do not pretend that Joy cannot associate with Beauty, but I will maintain that Joy is one of her most vulgar adornments, while Melancholy may be called her illustrious spouse—so much so that I can scarcely conceive (is my brain become a witch's mirror?) a type of Beauty which has nothing

to do with Sorrow. In pursuit of—others might say obsessed
by—those ideas, it may be supposed that I have difficulty in
not concluding from them that the most perfect type of manly
beauty is Satan—as Milton saw him.

Baudelaire. Fusées

The sun hides not the ocean, which is the dark side of this
earth, and which is two thirds of this earth. So therefore, that
mortal man who hath more of joy than sorrow in him, that
mortal man cannot be true—not true, or undeveloped. . . .
He who dodges hospitals and jails, and walks fast crossing
grave-yards, and would rather talk of operas than hell; calls
Cowper, Young, Pascal, Rousseau, poor devils all of sick men;
and throughout a care-free lifetime swears by Rabelais as
passing wise, and therefore jolly;—not that man is fitted to
sit down on tomb-stones, and break the green damp mould
with unfathomably wondrous Solomon.

Melville. Moby Dick xcvi

It is strange, too, that he most strongly enlisted my feelings
in behalf of the life of the seamen, when he depicted his more
terrible moments of suffering and despair. For the light side
of the painting I had a limited sympathy. My visions were of
shipwrecks, famines, of death and captivity among barbarian
hordes, of a lifetime dragged out in sorrow and tears upon
some gray and desolate wreck, in an ocean unfathomable and
unknown.

Poe. Gordon Pym

This is something new in the conception of the hero:
that he *ought* to be unhappy. Unhappiness, to the classical aesthetic hero, is the sign that he is ceasing to be

one; and to the classical ethical hero the sign that he has not yet become one.

There is also an agreement that the hero should be solitary, or if he does enter into relations with others, the relations should be very temporary. E.g. *Childe Harold:*

> Where rose the mountains, there to him were friends;
> Where rolled the ocean, thereon was his home;
> Where a blue sky, and glowing clime, extends,
> He had the passion and the power to roam;
> The desert, forest, cavern, breaker's foam,
> Were unto him companionship; they spake
> A mutual language, closer than the tome
> Of his land's tongue, which he would oft foresake
> For Nature's pages gloss'd by sunbeams on the lake.
>
> *   *   *
>
> But in Man's dwellings he became a thing
> Restless and worn, and stern and wearisome,
> Droop'd as a wild-born falcon with clipt wings
> To whom the boundless air alone were home.
> Then came his fit again, which to o'ercome
> As eagerly the barr'd-up bird will beat
> His breast and beak against the wiry dome
> Till the blood tinge his plumage, so the heat
> Of his impeded soul would through his bosom eat.
>
> III. 13. 15.

And Childe Harold says of himself:

> I have not loved the world, nor the world me;
> I have not flatter'd its rank breath, nor bow'd

> To the idolatries a patient knee,
> Nor conn'd my cheek to smiles, nor cried aloud
> In worship of an echo; in the crowd
> They could not deem me one of such; I stood
> Among them, but not of them, in a shroud
> Of thoughts which were not their thoughts, and still could,
> Had I not filed my mind, which thus itself subdued.

III. 113.

So Baudelaire:

Many friends, many gloves—for fear of the itch.
The Ancient Mariner has no use for marriage and though
he speaks favorably of praying in company:

> O sweeter than the marriage-feast
> 'Tis sweeter far to me,
> To walk together to the kirk
> With a goodly company!

he really thinks that the hermit's solitary moss cushion
in the wood is the proper church, and he himself wan-
ders about and is only related to others when he tells
them his story:

> I pass, like night, from land to land,
> I have strange power of speech;
> That moment that his face I see,
> I know the man that must hear me:
> To him my tale I teach.

He doesn't care whether or not the other wants to hear
it, and, the moment he has finished, has no further use
for him.

106

The same lack of any permanent interest in others and their opinions is equally apparent in those who are outwardly socially involved. Ahab is only interested in getting his crew to do what he wants; he is entirely indifferent to their opinion of him except insofar that he needs their approval or at least assent to carry out his scheme.

Goethe's Faust and Ibsen's Peer Gynt both meet a lot of people, but the whole point about these heroes is that they always leave the others behind.

The same is true of both Da Ponte-Mozart's *Don Giovanni* and Byron's *Don Juan*. At first sight it looks as if Don Giovanni, the seducer, must be intensely interested in women and in their opinion of him, but this is really not the case. He doesn't care what they look like, once is enough, and he has no wish to be remembered by them. Indeed, what causes his downfall is that some of them do. What he is really interested in, in fact, is not women, but his list of women seduced, the number of names in his private diary. Byron's Don Juan, who is always the seduced one, allows it to happen over and over again, not because he is interested in the lady but because it is a new experience to remember.

This again is novel. The classical aesthetic hero must command others' admiration as long as he can, the classical ethical hero must teach them all he can. If he were left alone without admirers or without pupils, he would cease to be himself.

THE GRIEVANCE

The classical aesthetic hero is pleased with the past, with his own record and his ancestor. If something tragic happens to him it is because he has been too pleased, too arrogantly happy.

With the Romantic Hero it is not so. The proof that he is the exceptional hero is that he comes of neurotic stock.

My ancestors, idiots or maniacs, in the solemn houses, all victims of terrible passions.

(Baudelaire. *Fusées*.)

or that his childhood was unhappy:

And lastly, if you are hungry or thirsty, there is someone who chases you.

(Rimbaud. *Les Illuminations*.)

And if, having surprised him in immodest acts of pity, his mother was alarmed, the profound tendernesses of the child fastened upon this astonishment. That's how it was. She had the blue-eyed look—which lies.

(Rimbaud. *Les Poètes de Sept Ans*.)

Something catastrophic has happened in the past to all of them. Even if, in the case of the Ancient Mariner, he alone is responsible for his catastrophe—through his criminal *acte gratuit* of shooting the Albatross—he only becomes a hero through it. Before that he was just anyone. He has long ago repented, done penance and been shriven by the hermit for his crime. Repentance, penance and pardon are usually thought of as putting an end to the matter. Now the sinner can forget the whole thing and be one of the family, of God's children, and of society. The Ancient Mariner does nothing of the sort. He has to confess over and over again to prove that he is interesting. He doesn't want to forget or to have others forget.

It is noteworthy that three of the Mariner heroes, the most dedicated, the most Quixotic, are dedicated to Revenge. Captain Ahab, to revenge the loss of his leg, Captain Nemo the loss of his wife and children, the hero of the *Voyage of Maeldune* the death of his father.

The avenging hero is, of course, a very ancient figure; but several significant changes have taken place.

In the *Oresteia*, for instance, Orestes avenges his father's death and is pursued by the Furies set on him by the ghost of his mother, and is finally absolved by the Divine Court of Justice. But it is important to note that

1) His murder of Clytemnestra is not a free choice of his own will, but a duty imposed upon him through his duty to his father.

2) The suffering he undergoes at the hands of the Furies is unexpected by him, is not due to anything in him, for they are set upon him from without.

3) He does not repent but is acquitted, on the grounds

109

that the duty to the father takes precedence over the duty to the mother.

4) He is a hero put into a tragic predicament, but if the situation were not tragic, he would still be a hero, only a happy one.

In most Elizabethan drama the revenge situation is similar. Shakespeare, however, had a new vision of the nature of revenge, and transformed the old Hamlet into the first hero of the romantic type. I.e., Shakespeare's Hamlet is made a hero by the situation in which he finds himself of having a mother who has committed adultery with his uncle, who has murdered his father. Before this happened he was no hero, just an ordinary pleasant young man. The result is that, instead of just avenging his father and getting it over with, he secretly cherishes the situation and cannot bear to end it, for who will he be then?

This conception of revenge as a vocation is made all the clearer when the revenge theme is combined with the quest theme. Traditionally, the quest is for some treasure, such as the water of life. Giants or dragons may get slain in the process because they stand between the hero and the treasure, but it is the obtaining of the treasure not the slaying of the dragon that is the hero's goal. The revenge as quest brings out the *value* of the hated object to the hero.

The Romantic Avenger Hero, in fact, is a person who is in dread of not having a vocation and yet is unable to choose one for himself as Don Quixote does (the proof that Don Quixote's decision to save the world is his own is that he has no idea what the world is like), and so has to be given it from without.

"My injury," he says, "is not an injury *to* me; it *is* me. If I cancel it out by succeeding in my vengeance, I shall not know who I am and will have to die. I cannot live without it." So not only does he cherish the memory of a catastrophic injury, but also he is not lured forward by the hope of happiness at some future date.

That Ethical Hero of the Enlightenment, Prince Tamino in the *Magic Flute*, braves suffering, the ordeal by fire and water, because he knows that on the other side of it wait the Palace of Wisdom and the Princess Pamina. The Religious Hero, Don Quixote, may accept suffering in the cause of duty cheerfully without thinking of any reward, but he would much rather not suffer, does not congratulate himself on suffering nor deliberately seek it.

But the Romantic Hero does not expect any ultimate relief. The hero of *Bateau Ivre* is not motivated by any hope of reaching the Islands of the Blessed; the Baker more than half suspects that the Snark may be a Boojum. Nor does Ahab believe for a moment that if he succeeds in killing the White Whale, he will be any happier.

Before discussing why this should be so, we should first see the hero in relation to those who are not, and

111

perhaps the simplest way to do this is to take one group, the crew of the *Pequod*.

ISHMAEL-MELVILLE

Ishmael cannot properly be called a member of the crew; for, from the moment that he steps on board, he only speaks or is spoken to once more when after his first ducking (baptism) he makes his will, i.e., consciously accepts the absolute finality of his commitment. From then on, he becomes simply the recording consciousness, the senses and the mind through which we experience everything.

This suggests that if we are identified with him then, we should also identify ourselves with him during the prologue when he does have a certain personal existence.

One day in Manhattan Ishmael resolves to go whaling. To this resolution he is pushed from behind by the need to escape from a spiritual condition of spleen and powerlessness—Manhattan is for him the *selva oscura* of the *Divine Comedy* and the Sargasso Sea of the Ancient Mariner; and he is lured from in front by a vague but haunting image. He has never consciously heard of Moby Dick yet:

in the wild conceits that swayed me to my purpose, two and two there floated into my inmost soul, endless processions of the whale, and, midmost of them all, one grand hooded phantom, like a snow hill in the air.

(1)

112

But between this initial resolve and the actual decision, the irrevocable commitment of signing on the *Pequod*, he has a preliminary journey to make, during which he is subjected to various initiations from any of which he could draw back and return to the city.

He begins to move away from the safe centre of normal routine, convention and status (he has been a schoolmaster, i.e., a conventional authority) towards the edge of the land to the port New Bedford. The first test is a shock of fright. Imagining it to be an inn, i.e., a place of shelter and friendly companionship, he pushes open the door of *The Trap* and finds himself in a Negro church when the minister is preaching about hell, the wailing and gnashing of teeth. This is a warning that in his state of spleen from which he is trying to escape, it is easy to take a wrong turning—into despair. He rejects this and enters the Spouter Inn whose proprietor has the ominous name of Coffin. (It is finally a coffin that saves him from drowning—death and rebirth are two aspects of the same thing. Who would save his life must lose it.) Here he has a brief glimpse of the Handsome Sailor, Bulkington, who will play no part in *Moby Dick*, but will appear as a protagonist in a later work of Melville's under the name of Billy Budd, and the whole Queequeg episode begins.

Ishmael is a white man and a Presbyterian: Queequeg is a South-Sea Islander and a Pagan, formerly a cannibal. The Christian world is the world of consciousness, i.e., the ethically superior world which knows the truth, both the artistic and scientific truths and the moral truth that one should love one's neighbor as oneself.

The pagan world is the unconscious world, which does not know the truth. The cannibalism it practises is a symbol of self-love, of treating one's neighbor as existing solely for one's own advantage. Queequeg left his island in order to become conscious of the truth, only to discover that those who are conscious of it do not obey it, and so has decided to live as a pagan in the Christian world.

Ishmael, like us, has two preconceived notions.

1) That men who are not white are ugly, i.e., in a physical sense, aesthetically inferior. He has just had that notion reinforced by seeing the handsome white Bulkington.
2) That pagans cannot obey the Christian commandment to love one's neighbor as oneself, because they have never heard the Word of the true God, i.e., they are ethically inferior.

Ishmael is disabused of both notions. He admits that Queequeg is beautiful, and that he loves his neighbor, in fact, more than most Christians. When on the short voyage from New Bedford to Nantucket Queequeg rescues from drowning—again a test of Ishmael's courage (can he face the possibility of drowning?)—the man who has just insulted him, saying "It's a mutual joint-stock world in all meridians. We cannibals must help these Christians," he exhibits Christian forgiveness and Christian *agape* without the slightest effort. He is a doer of the Word who has never heard the Word.

By accepting Queequeg—the symbolic act of acceptance is his joining in the worship of Queequeg's idol—Ishmael proves himself worthy of the voyage.

The last tests are the mysterious warning by Elijah not to sail on the *Pequod*, another test of courage, and the encounter with the owners, Captains Peleg and Bildad.

This pair are Quakers, i.e., people who consciously believe in applying the absolute law of love in time and the world. No man who is not a saint can do this; Ishmael has first to be made conscious through this pair of the discrepancy between Heaven's time and Jerusalem time, and then to be warned against falling into either of the two temptations which follow the moment one is so conscious, either of frivolity, i.e., taking the contradiction too lightly, which is what Peleg does, or, more seriously, of hypocrisy, i.e., of pretending that there is no contradiction and that one is living by Heaven's time, which is what Bildad does. Bildad's besetting vice is avarice, which is the spiritual version of cannibalism. He does not eat men, but he exploits them to the death. Avarice is worse than cannibalism because the latter is limited by natural appetite —you cannot eat more than a certain amount of flesh— but avarice has no limits—there is no end to the accumulation of money.

115

FATHER MAPPLE'S SERMON

Standing apart from Ishmael's other tests is Father Mapple's Sermon. This is not, as has sometimes been said, a magnificent irrelevance, but an essential clue to the meaning of the whole book. The story of Jonah is the story of a voyage undertaken for the wrong reasons, of learning repentance through suffering and a final acceptance of duty. Jonah has ethical authority, i.e., he knows the Word; he is called upon to become more than that, to become an ethical hero with absolute passion, i.e., a religious hero; he flees from the divine command out of aesthetic pride, a fear that he will not be listened to and admired, not be an aesthetic hero. He is punished for his refusal by being confronted with the really aesthetically great, the storm and the whale, compared with which the greatest emperor is a puny weakling, and then, in the whale's belly, he is deprived of even the one gift he had, his ability to hear the Word. Humbled, he does not despair but repents and trusts in the God whom he can no longer hear. God forgives him, he is cast up on the land, and sets off to fulfil his vocation.

In drawing the moral, Father Mapple says two apparently contradictory things.

1) If we obey God, we must disobey ourselves; and it is in this disobeying of ourselves, wherein the hardness of obeying God consists.

2) Delight is to him—a far, far upward and inward delight—who against the proud gods and commo-

dores of this earth ever stands forth his own inexo-
rable self.

This is the same thing that the Button-Moulder says to
Peer Gynt:

> To be one's self is to slay one's self
> But as perhaps that explanation
> Is thrown away on you, let's say,
> To follow out, in everything,
> What the Master's intention was.
>
> (v. 9.)

Man's being is a copulative relation between a subject
ego and a predicate self. The ego is aware of the self as
given, already there in the world, finite, derived, along
with, related and comparable to other beings. It is
further aware of the self not only as existing but also
as potential, as not fully actual but as a self which
becomes itself.

Being of itself unaware of its potentialities, the self
cannot become itself of itself, cannot initiate anything;
all it desires is to be in equilibrium, a self-enjoying, self-
sufficient self: the responsibility for self-realisation lies
with the ego which can decide; the self can only welcome
or resist the decision when it is taken.

The ego, on the other hand, has no potentialities,
only existence. Further, it is isolated; it cannot compare its egoship with other egos, as it can compare the
self it is related to with other selves.

117

The desire of the ego is a double one. As freely owning a self, it desires a self of which it can approve. As solitary it desires to be approved of for the self it has. This approval must have absolute authority, for the approval of finite beings whom the ego can see are not self-existent posits an ultimate authority which approves of their approval, i.e., the ego desires a God.

The ego, therefore, has three tasks:

1) To know the self and the world, as they exist now.
2) To know the true God and what He requires the ego to realise in the self as he knows it.
3) To obey these commands.

The ego may err in three ways:

1) It may refuse to look honestly at its given self and prefer a vague or a fantastic conception to the truth. The temptation to do so arises from the fear that if it should know the truth about the self, it would find that it had a self of which it did not approve, i.e., not the sort of self it would like to have to develop.
2) It may prefer a false god to the true God. The temptation to do this arises out of a fear that if it knew the true God, the ego would encounter disapproval. A false god or idol is always one which the ego believes it can manage through magic; upon whose approval, therefore, it can, if it is smart enough, depend.
3) Knowing the self and what God requires to realise in the self, it may disobey negatively out of weak-

ness, yielding to the opposition of the self to change, or positively out of defiance, in assertion of its autonomy.

THE VOYAGE OF THE PEQUOD

The voyage of the *Pequod* is one voyage for Ishmael and with him us, and another for the rest of the crew.

For us the voyage signifies the exploration of the self and the world, of potential essences. Nothing happens to us, we survive, and we are the same people at the end as at the beginning except that we know ourselves and others better. We had to be tested first to see whether we were capable of such an exploration; once we have passed the tests, we have nothing to do but record.

For the rest of the crew, however, it is not the voyage of self-inspection before the act, but the act of historical existence itself. They learn nothing about themselves, but they are changed before our eyes, and reveal themselves unwittingly in what they say and do.

When we have finished the book, we realise why Father Mapple's sermon was put in where it was: in order that we might know the moral presuppositions by which we are to judge the speeches and actions of Ahab and the rest.

The crew of the *Pequod* are a society whose function is to kill whales. As such each has a specialised function of his own, arranged in a hierarchy of authority.

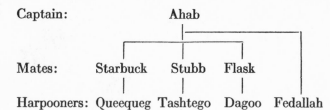

Captain: Ahab

Mates: Starbuck   Stubb   Flask

Harpooners: Queequeg   Tashtego   Dagoo   Fedallah

Then the crowd of seamen who man the whale-boats, of whom one or two appear for a moment, such as the old Manx sailor. Standing apart from them because their special functions are only indirectly connected with whales are:

> Pip, Ahab's cabin boy
> Perth, the Blacksmith
> Carpenter

In their motives for going on the voyage:
    Ahab wants to kill one particular whale.
    The Blacksmith wishes to escape his memories.
    The Carpenter wants to carpenter.
    Pip doesn't want to go because he is terrified, but has no option. The rest have a common motive which makes them a community, they want to earn their living, in a way for which they are fitted and which they enjoy. Since they are doing what they like and are good at they are a happy community, and for them killing whales is morally permissible and indeed a much better job than most. It may sometimes tempt to unnecessary cruelty—as when Flask deliberately pricks the abscess of the old whale—but it encourages courage

and democratic comradeship—the atmosphere on the *Pequod* is very different from that of the *Neversink*.

They are therefore in the right in going on the voyage. The only ones who should not have gone are firstly Ahab, because he has passed beyond killing whales in general, and secondly Pip, who lacks the courage which for whaling is essential, just as Captain De Deer of the *Jungfrau* and the captain of the *Rosebud* lack the necessary knowledge and skill.

THE FOUR SQUIRES

The four squires are representatives of the four non-white Pagan races.

Queequeg is	a South Sea Islander
Tashtego	a North American Indian
Dagoo	an African Negro
Fedallah	an Asiatic

Queequeg, Tashtego and Dagoo form a trio related to and contrasted with the white trio Starbuck, Stubb, and Flask, i.e., the three untormented by the problems of consciousness and the three who in different ways fail to live up to the challenge of consciousness.

Queequeg and Fedallah are opposites in their relation to Christianity. I.e., Queequeg is the unconscious Christian, Fedallah is the unconscious anti-Christian, the tempter of Ahab. In the Biblical story of Ahab, the Lord sends a lying spirit to entice him to his death. Such is Fedallah, who is Ahab's shadow and makes the *Macbeth-*

121

like prophecies which finally persuade Ahab that he will succeed in killing the White Whale and survive. Fedallah alone, though he has not suffered Ahab's catastrophe, intuitively shares Ahab's attitude. Like Ahab he is a fire-worshipper.

He was such a creature as civilized, domestic people in the temperate zone only see in their dreams, and that but dimly; but the like of whom now and then glide among the unchanging Asiatic communities, especially the Oriental isles to the east of the continent—those insulated, immemorial, unalterable countries, which even in these modern days still preserve much of the ghostly aboriginalness of earth's primal generations, when the memory of the first man was a distinct recollection, and all men his descendants, unknowing whence he came, eyed each other as real phantoms, and asked of the sun and the moon why they were created and to what end; when though, according to Genesis, the angels indeed consorted with the daughters of men, the devils also, add the uncanonical Rabbins, indulged in mundane amours.

(L)

One thing all four have in common, a magnificent physique. To the romantics as a whole consciousness is usually held to upset the psychosomatic balance and to bring either ugliness or sickness. Those who are both beautiful and healthy belong to

> *ces époques nues*
> *Dont Phoebus se plaisait à dorer les statues.*
> *Alors l'homme et la femme en leur agilité*
> *Jouissaient sans mensonge et sans anxiété,*

Et, le ciel amoureux leur caressant l'échine,
Exerçaient la santé de leur noble machine.
(Baudelaire)

In Father Mapple's terms, all four are themselves; but, since they are unconscious, i.e., since they have not begun Ishmael's voyage nor been called by the Lord like Jonah, they are only potentially themselves. Queequeg is not only himself but obeys God without having to disobey himself. Fedallah obeys himself and the Devil, i.e., denies the true God.

THE THREE MATES

None of the three mates is an evil man. All are physically brave, loyal and free from malice. Yet all suffer from spiritual sloth, which is a form of cowardice, so that none is his complete self; all have refused to grow up. They have, as it were, started on Ishmael's voyage and then tried to draw back, but that voyage is like a sea voyage in that once the boat has left the shore, you cannot get off, you can only play the child's game of "let's pretend we are on shore." Each of them in his own way takes ship from Tarshish to flee from the presence of the Lord.

STARBUCK

Starbuck has gone farthest and is the most fitted for the voyage so that he suffers most from his refusal to go all the way.

He has a religious reverence for life and death; he knows that the fear of the Lord is the beginning of wisdom. That is why he will have no man in his boat who is not afraid of the whale.

He has mature self-control and authority in excitement.

He did not say much to his crew, nor did his crew say anything to him. Only the silence of the boat was at intervals startlingly pierced by one of his peculiar whispers, now harsh with command, now soft with entreaty.

(XLVIII)

He alone of the three has an inkling that Ahab's soul is in danger, and therefore looks at him not only with mingled fear and admiration but with pity and love.

He can tell Ahab the truth, as when he rebukes him for seeking "vengeance on a dumb brute that simply smote thee from blindest instinct," or again "Moby Dick seeks thee not. It is thou, thou that madly seekest him."

He knows that in obeying Ahab he is disobeying God, yet before Ahab's passion his knowledge and righteous fear are powerless: "I think I see his impious end, but feel that I must help him to it. 'Tis my miserable office to obey, rebelling."

Because fear may be the right way to begin, but it is not enough to go on with. For in the fear which is reverence is mixed the fear which is cowardice, the fear that the whole truth may be too much to encounter, that too much will be asked of me, that in fact God will not add His grace to one's own powers. Thus, Starbuck remains in the childish religious state of believing in omens like the Squid. "Almost rather had I seen Moby Dick and fought him, than to have seen thee, thou white ghost." He dare not look at the Doubloon too closely. "This coin speaks wisely, mildly, truly, but still sadly to me. I will quit it, lest Truth shake me falsely." And looking down into the Ocean on a beautiful calm day he sees belief and reason, faith and knowledge as contradictory. He keeps to his belief but at the cost of refusing to experience. His faith is insufficient for that.

Loveliness unfathomable as ever lover saw in his young bride's eye!—Tell me not thou of thy teeth-tiered sharks, and thy kidnapping cannibal ways. Let faith oust fact; let fancy oust memory; I look deep down and do believe.

(CXIV)

STUBB

It is characteristic of Stubb that, of the three of them, he should be the one who is always describing himself to himself to reassure himself.

"I guess he's got what some folks ashore call a conscience, it's a kind of Tic-Dolly-Row they say—worse than a tooth-ache. Well, well, I don't know what it is, but the Lord keep me from catching it. Damn me, it's worth a fellow's while to be born into the world, if only to fall asleep. Damn me, but all things are queer, come to think of 'em. But that's against my prin-

125

ciples. Think not, is my eleventh commandment, and sleep when you can is my twelfth."

(XXIX)

"A laugh's the wisest easiest answer to all that's queer."

"I know not all that may be coming but be it what it will, I'll go to it laughing."

"It's against my religion to get mad."

"I am Stubb and Stubb has his history but here Stubb takes oaths that he has always been jolly."

For the comic always involves standing outside a situation, and so a man who makes a religion of the comic must be humorously self-regarding.

A man may laugh for pleasure or joy. Pleasure or joy are not comic, and the appropriate response is song, i.e., the expression of gratitude and praise. If a man lacks the gift of song, then he may laugh as a substitute. The substitute is acceptable because there is no suffering involved, except the comic contradiction of being unable to sing in a situation demanding song and in which laughter is actually ridiculous.

For what is the comic? The comic is a contradiction that does not involve suffering, either directly in the subject or indirectly by sympathetic identification with those involved in the contradiction.

There is, however, a particular religious form of the comic in which suffering is involved, i.e., a man may laugh at suffering on condition that 1) it is he who suffers, 2) he knows that, ironically, this suffering is really a sign that he is in the truth, that he who suffers is really blest.

But the suffering must be real, i.e., not enjoyed. When Stubb thinks about his wife, he says:

"What's my juicy little pear at home doing now? Crying its eyes out?—Giving a party to the last arrived harpooners, I dare say, gay as a frigate's pennant, and so am I—fa, la!"

(xxxix)

It looks at first as if this might be humorous resignation, but the end of the sentence gives him away. He is not suffering at the thought of his wife's infidelity, either because he no longer loves her, or because he is not really imagining a real scene, but a comic French farce in a theatre.

A man who makes a religion out of the comic is unable to face suffering. He is bound to deny it or to look the other way. When Stubb looks at the Doubloon, he abstracts from it the features which can fit into his view of life and ignores the rest.

"There's a sermon now, writ in high heaven, and the sun goes through it every year, and yet comes out of it all alive and hearty."

Stubb, however, is not soulless, i.e., he knows that suffering and mysteries which are not comic exist:

"I wonder whether the world is anchored anywhere, if she is she swings with an uncommon long cable."

127

He senses, where Flask does not, the demonic qualities of Fedallah; but his solution is to put him away where he can't be seen:

"Who's fond of the devil except the old governor who dares not catch him and put him down in double darbies as he deserves."

And he gives himself away in his dream about Ahab, which is a terror dream, but on waking he does not meet this fact but says: "The best thing you can do, Flask, is to let that old man alone; never speak to him, whatever he says."

Starbuck fears God; Stubb fears suffering. Starbuck knows what he fears; Stubb doesn't, which makes him all the more insistent in his defence. As in a characteristic moment of frankness—the frankness itself is a defensive theatre—Stubb confesses to Starbuck: "I am not a brave man; never said I was a brave man; I am a coward; and I sing to keep up my spirits. And I tell you what it is, Mr. Starbuck, there's no way to stop my singing in this world but to cut my throat."

When he does not or cannot sing, he turns away like a child from the frightening world to the comforting breast, i.e., to his pipe, which is never out of his mouth. The sight of the whale's blood is slightly disquieting to him so that he substitutes a pleasant image: "Would now it were old Orleans Whiskey," and his last thought in the moment of death is food. "Oh Flask, for one red cherry ere we die."

In his relations to his neighbor, he substitutes good-fellowship for love. "I never hurt when I hit, except when I hit a whale or something of that sort." His method of talking to his boat crew is one of good-tempered banter: "Pull, pull, my fine hearts—alive; pull, my little ones . . . Pull, then, do pull; never mind the brimstone—devils are good fellows enough."

The difficulty about good-fellowship as a principle of social conduct is that one's neighbor must also be a good-fellow, i.e., not a sufferer. Thus Stubb, who prides himself on his kindness, is the one who becomes guilty of destroying an innocent boy's sanity, for he cannot understand Pip's kind of fear, which cannot be laughed off. He does not guess what the consequences of leaving Pip in the water will be, because he has never really looked at him.

The best comment on Stubb is an aphorism of Kafka's:

You can hold back from the suffering of the world, you have free permission to do so and it is in accordance with your nature, but perhaps this very holding back is the one suffering that you could have avoided . . .

FLASK

Flask is the least sympathetic of the three. Stubb, when confronted with mystery and suffering, looks the other way; Flask denies that it exists. Stubb would never laugh at the spectacle of a wrecked boat. Flask

129

does. In relation to others he has the child's shameless-
ness and lack of dignity. For instance, his conduct in a
whale-boat:

"Lay me on—lay me on! O Lord, Lord! but I shall go stark,
staring mad: See! see that white water!" And so shouting, he
pulled his hat from his head, and stamped up and down on it;
then picking it up, flirted it far off upon the sea; and finally
fell to rearing and plunging in the boat's stern like a crazed
colt from the prairie.

He is also the only one whom Peleg warns against forni-
cation.

Towards animals he is cruel like a child.

"A nice spot. Just let me prick him there once."

Towards the mysterious, however, instead of a child's
reverence, he has developed the underdog's Philistin-
ism; he trivialises everything. The whale is only a
magnified water-rat; the doubloon is only a round
thing made of gold worth sixteen dollars or nine hundred
and sixty cigars.

His reaction to imminent death is equally characteristic. Starbuck says, "May God stand by me now";
Stubb thinks of food; Flask thinks of his mother and
money: "I hope my poor mother has drawn my part-
pay ere this; if not, few coppers will now come to her
for the voyage."

THE CARPENTER AND THE
BLACKSMITH

Something has been said about these two in the first chapter, and there is not much to add here. If the harpooners have not started on Ishmael's voyage, and if the mates have started and tried to escape, for these all voyages are over. They are not children, nor childish, but senile. What catastrophe happened we do not know, for though we know that Perth's life went smash through drink, we do not know what made him a drunkard. Whatever the cause, though, they have lost themselves, and only exist in the tasks they are given to do. While Queequeg and Co. are potential selves, not consciously actual, the Carpenter and the Blacksmith have lost their actual selves, and there are no potentialities left. They are simply passively waiting for physical death to be superimposed on the spiritual death which has already taken place.

PIP

Pip is more significant, as his despair is dialectically related to Ahab's. Between them they represent the two opposite kinds of despair which Kierkegaard defines as:

The despair of weakness. i.e., The despair of willing despairingly not to be oneself

and

The despair of defiance. i.e., The despair of willing despairingly to be oneself.

131

Pip is a slave, i.e., the one who has no authority, aesthetic, ethical or religious. He should never have been taken on this voyage at all, and he is innocent, for he never wanted to, knowing that he lacks the qualities required:

"Have mercy on this small Black boy down here. Preserve him from all men that have no bowels to feel fear."

His proper place is in a fairy story where fairy godmothers and animals assist him against all probability to vanquish the giant (who kills himself by mistake) and marry the Princess. But it has not been so. Papageno has been made to go through the ordeal and it has destroyed him.

He is bound to Ahab because they have both suffered a catastrophe, Ahab through his own deliberate original attack on the whale, Pip through the thoughtless action of the decent fellow Stubb. But Ahab is the exception, for whom exceptional situations are made; Pip is not. Ahab, knowing that he is the exception, is outraged by a catastrophe he was not powerful enough to command; Pip is outraged by not being up to the command of the situation. Thus Ahab's madness is directed against the whale; Pip's is directed against himself. "Seek not Pip who's now been missing long. If ye find Pip, tell all the Antilles he's a runaway; a coward, a coward, a coward. Tell them he jumped from a whaleboat. I'd never beat my tambourine over Pip, and hail him general." Having lost himself, he can only exist through the self of another, and where should he find that but in Ahab, the defiant self, so that he cannot bear to be out of sight, and he only exists in obeying him.

Here he this instant stood; I stand in his air,—but I'm alone. Now were even Pip here I could endure it, but he's missing . . . let's try the door. What? neither lock, nor bolt, nor bar; and yet there's no opening it. It must be the spell; he told me to stay here . . . Hist! above there. I hear ivory— Oh, master! master! I am indeed down-hearted when you walk over me. But here I'll stay, though this stern strikes rocks; and they bulge through; and oysters come to join me.

(CXXIX)

Ahab on his side is bound to Pip, and to no one else, not even Starbuck. As the conscious defiant despairer, he recognises that Pip is his antitype and envies Pip's humility as Pip admires his strength. "There's that in thee, poor lad, which I feel too curing for my malady. Like cures like; and for this hunt, my malady becomes my most desired health."

If each could have had the qualities of the other added to his own, when they encountered catastrophe, i.e., if Ahab had had Pip's humility as well as his own strength and vice versa, both would have been saved.

A H A B

Kierkegaard defines defiant despair as follows:

. . . with hatred for existence it wills to be itself, to be itself in terms of its misery; it does not even in defiance or defiantly

will to be itself, but to be itself in spite . . . Whereas the
weak despairer will not hear about what comfort eternity has
for him, so neither will such a despairer hear about it, but for
a different reason, namely, because this comfort would be the
destruction of him as an objection against the whole of existence. It is (to describe it figuratively) as if an author were to
make a slip of the pen, and that this clerical error became
conscious of being such—perhaps it was no error but in a far
higher sense was an essential constituent in the whole ex-
position—it is then as if this clerical error would revolt against
the author, out of hatred for him were to forbid him to correct
it, and were to say, "No, I will not be erased, I will stand as a
witness against thee, that thou art a very poor writer."

(*Sickness unto Death*)

Of this despair, Ahab is a representation, perhaps the
greatest in literature.

Before he was born there were prophecies of some
extraordinary destiny, which caused his mother to
name him Ahab, after the son of Omri, of whom it is
written in the book of Kings that he "did evil in the
sight of the Lord above all that were before him," that
reared up an altar for Baal, that he made a grove, and
constructed an ivory house.

He himself declares that the prophecy was that he
should be dismembered. Now a prophecy is either true
or false, and in either case the only thing to do is to
ignore it. If it is true, then it will happen and must be
accepted when it occurs, and it is defiance either to try
to make it happen or to try to avoid it. If it is false, it
will not happen, and if one makes it happen one is not

really fulfilling a prophecy at all but doing what one has chosen to do.

As a symbol of his uniqueness, he is distinguished from the rest of mankind by a scar. About this there is a mystery. An Indian relative of Tashtego's says that Ahab was forty before he received it; the old Manx sailor, on the other hand, declares that Ahab was born with it. Ahab himself makes a mysterious statement during the thunderstorm:

> "Oh! thou clear spirit of clear fire, whom on these seas I as Persian once did worship, till in the sacramental act so burned by thee, that to this hour I bear the scar."
>
> (CXIX)

Whether he was born marked, whether he received it by chance, or in some mysterious blasphemous rite is left vague. All we know for certain is that before his encounter with Moby Dick he was an exceptional man, an aesthetic hero.

So he encounters Moby Dick and loses a leg. That this is a castration symbol is emphasized by the story of how shortly before the present voyage he was found insensible in the street "by some unknown, and seemingly inexplicable, unimaginable casualty, his ivory limb having been so violently displaced that it had stake-wise smitten, and all but pierced his groin." * It

---

* Ahab's rival as an idolator of Moby Dick, Gabriel, worships the whale as the incarnation of the Shaker God, for whom the primal sin is sexual intercourse.

is possible to attach too much importance to this as also to the sexual symbolism of the Whale as being at once the *vagina dentata* and the Beast with two backs or the parents-in-bed. The point is that the sexual symbolism is in its turn symbolic of the aesthetic, i.e., the Oedipus fantasy is a representation in aesthetic terms of the fantasy of being a self-originating god, i.e., of the ego (Father) begetting itself on the self (Mother), and castration is the ultimate symbol of aesthetic weakness, of not being an aesthetic hero.

Ahab, then, the exceptional hero, suffers a tragic fall in the Greek sense, he is reduced to being lower than the average. In a Greek story this would be a punishment by the gods for hybris, and would come at the end of the book. Here, however, it comes before the book starts, so we must take it differently. How should Ahab react? Repent of his past pride? Perhaps, but the important thing is the future. What is the catastrophe telling him to become? Here again we can only answer negatively and say, "At least, not to go on whaling." One might hazard a guess and say, "To will to become nobody in particular in an aesthetic sense," i.e., to be a happy husband and father, to enter the cloister, the actual symbol does not concern us; the decisive difference is between the kind of individuality which is *being* what others are not, and that defined as "*becoming* what one wills or God wills for one."

Ahab does turn into such an individual but in a negative sense. He neither says, "I am justly punished" if he has been guilty nor "Though He slay me yet will I trust in Him" but "Thou art guilty and shalt be punished." His nature or self certainly does not wish to go rushing off in his aged maimed state round the world chasing a whale. It wants, as he himself admits, peace, family and, above all, happiness. It is as if, knowing that this is also what God wills him to become, he, his ego, defiantly wills to be always at every moment miserable. His extra wounding of himself, mentioned above, may well have been, at least unconsciously, not an accident, but a goading of himself to remember his vow. It is interesting to note the occasion during the voyage when he breaks his leg, jumping off the *Enderby*, whose captain has also lost an arm to Moby Dick without despairing and whose doctor ascribes Moby Dick's apparent malice to clumsiness. The example of sanity with authority is too much for Ahab, and he must again goad himself to his resolution.

So in defiance he takes his vow: "I now prophesy that I will dismember my dismemberer. Now then, be this prophet and the fulfiller one. That's more than ye, ye great gods, ever were."

The defiant man and the obedient man use the same words "It is not I but Fate," but their meaning is opposite.

The path to my fixed purpose is laid with iron rails, whereon my soul is grooved to run . . . The whole act's immutably decreed. I am the Fates' Lieutenant. I act under orders.

So too, as we follow him on his unnecessary voyage, unnecessary because he has been on it before and nothing new, as he well knows, can happen to him, only, possibly, to the whale, we watch him enact every ritual of the dedicated Don Quixote life of the Religious Hero, only for negative reasons.

His first act is to throw away his pipe, an act of ascetic renunciation. But what should be done, so as not to be distracted from the task set one by God, is done to prevent distraction from a task set by himself.

Next he sets up the Doubloon which is to be a prize for whoever sights Moby Dick first. The motive is simple enough—to inspire the crew in terms of their interests to work for his—actually, however, Ahab hasn't the slightest intention of letting anyone but himself be the first. At the same time he makes the harpooners swear an oath to pursue Moby Dick to the death.

Now an oath is an individual's commitment of his individual future. It is an aesthetic form of the ethical, for if later its fulfillment should turn out to involve violating ethics, the one who took the oath cannot release himself, which can only be done by the individual or his representative before whom the oath was made. It is right therefore to take an oath about a certain direction of the will, e.g., to vow at the altar that one will love one's wife till death. It would be all wrong to take an oath about a particular future act, e.g., that one will give one's wife a pound of candy every week,

138

for the act which at this moment is an expression of one's love may not be tomorrow; she may get diabetes.

When it comes to persuading another to take an oath, not only must there be no coercion, the other must be completely free to refuse, but also he must understand exactly what is going on; he must have the right motive. Ahab violates these conditions both for himself and for the harpooners. He exercises his authority as captain, he weakens their will with drink, and they have no motives for taking the oath at all, nor could they understand his if he told them.

Later he goes further and baptises his harpoon itself. This is a perversion of the Knight Errant's act of dedicating his arms, so that he shall remember not to dishonor them. Ahab's act, however, is a pure act of black magic, an attempt to compel objects to do his will.

Three other acts are worth mention. He throws away the ship's quadrant with the words: "Science! Curse thee, thou vain toy; and cursed be all the things that cast man's eyes aloft to the heavens. . . . Level by nature to this earth's horizon are the glances of men's eyes; not shot from the crown of his head, as if God had meant him to gaze on his firmament." This is the defiant inversion in pride of the humility which resists the pride of reason, the theologian's temptation to think that knowledge of God is more important than obeying Him.

Next he places the child Pip in his place in the captain's cabin and takes the humble position of the lookout, an inversion of "He who would be greatest among you, let him be as the least."

Lastly, in refusing the call for help of his neighbor, the captain of the *Rachel*, whom he has known in Nantucket and who asks him to help look for his young son, he counterfeits the text:

If any man come to me and hate not his father and mother and wife and children and brethren and sisters, yea and his own life also, he cannot be my disciple.

His whole life, in fact, is one of taking up defiantly a cross he is not required to take up. Consequently, the normal reactions to pleasure and pain are reversed for him. Painful situations like the typhoon he welcomes, pleasant and happy ones like the calm day he regards as temptations. This is a counterfeit version of the saints' acceptance of suffering and distrust of pleasure. The aesthetic hero reacts normally, in that it is pleasure that tempts him to do wrong, and if he is doing wrong, suffering will dissuade him. Thus the hero of *The Voyage of Maeldune*, who is also bent on vengeance but not for himself but for his father, is brought to his senses by suffering, i.e., by the disasters that happen to his men on each of the islands they come to. The Religious Hero, however, is related in exactly the opposite way, and if his god be his own defiant will, it is pain that tempts him further, and pleasure that could save him.

In the same way Queequeg is a saint, but he is not

the Christ incarnate, the second Adam, for, though he goes down with the rest of the crew, he does not suffer uniquely as an individual. For Melville's treatment of the Religious Hero and the Devil or the negative Religious Hero in their absolute form, we must now turn to his last work, *Billy Budd*.

BILLY BUDD

If, when we finish reading *Billy Budd*, we are left with questions which we feel have been raised but not answered, if so to speak the equation has not come out to a finite number, as in a work of art it should, this is not due to any lack of talent on Melville's part, but to the insolubility of the religious paradox in aesthetic terms.

For any writer who attempts a portrait of the Christlike is faced with the following problems. His central figure

a) must be innocent of sin, yet a man like us in all things tempted as we are. If he is given any aesthetic advantages, he at once ceases to be the God-Man and becomes the Man-God, the Aesthetic Hero, Hercules, who must be admired, but cannot be imitated. His sinlessness must be the result of faith, not of fortune.

b) He must be shown as failing in a worldly sense, i.e., as coming into collision with the law of this world, otherwise there is no proof that his sinlessness is due, not to faith, but to mere worldly prudence.

141

c) Failure and suffering, however, are in themselves no proof of faith, because the collision with the law may equally well be the result of pride and sin. The crucified Christ is flanked by two crucified thieves.

d) The suffering must at one and the same time be willed and not-willed. If it seems entirely against the will of the sufferer, he becomes pathetic, if it seems entirely brought about by his own actions, he becomes tragic, and it is impossible to distinguish between pride and faith as the cause of his suffering.

We have seen how Cervantes tackled these problems. His ironically comic approach solved all the problems, I think, except the last one. As long as Don Quixote is mad, the suffering is not quite real, but if he becomes sane and still resists he becomes tragically proud.

Melville, on the other hand, solves this problem. The Passion of Billy Budd is convincing, but fails in respects where Cervantes succeeds, and the ways in which he fails are interesting for the light they throw on the romantic conception of life. Like many other romantics Melville seems to hold:

1) That innocence and sinlessness are identical, or rather perhaps that only the innocent, i.e., those who have never known the law, can be sinless. Once a man becomes conscious, he becomes a sinner. As long as he is not conscious of guilt, what he does is not sin. This is to push St. Paul's remark "Except I had known the Law, I had not known sin" still further to mean that "Except I had known sin, I

would not have sinned." * Thus when Billy Budd first appears he is the Prelapsarian Adam:

> Billy Budd in many respects was little more than a sort of upright barbarian, much such perhaps as Adam presumably might have been ere the urbane Serpent wriggled himself into his company.

> He may have done things which in a conscious person would be sin—there appears to have been a certain Bristol Molly—but he feels no guilt.

2) That the unconscious and innocent are marked by great physical beauty, and therefore that the beautiful are sinless. This is true for Billy Budd as it was for Bulkington and Queequeg.

If the story were to be simply the story of the Fall, i.e., the story of how the Devil (Claggart) tempted Adam (Budd) into the knowledge of good and evil, this would not matter, but Melville wants Budd also to be the Second Adam, the sinless victim who suffers voluntarily for the sins of the whole world. But in order to be that he must know what sin is, or else his suffering is not redemptive, but only one more sin on our part. Further, as long as Billy Budd is only the Prelapsarian Adam, our nostalgic image of what we would still be if we had not fallen, his beauty is a perfectly adequate

---

* In the Barrister's dream in *The Hunting of the Snark* the pig is charged with deserting its sty, i.e., the crime is not the eating of the tree but the expulsion from Eden. The Snark who is officially the counsel for the defence is also the accuser-judge and the sentence is a repetition of the offence. "Transportation for life."

143

symbol but the moment he becomes the Second Adam, the saving example whom we all should follow, this beauty becomes an illegitimate aesthetic advantage. The flaw of the stammer will not quite do, for this is only an aesthetic weakness, not a deliberate abandonment of advantages. It succeeds in making Billy Budd the innocent who "as a sheep before the shearer is dumb so openeth he not his mouth," but it makes his dumbness against his will not with it. We can never look like that, any more than, once we have become conscious, we can go back to unconsciousness, so how can we imitate his example? He becomes an aesthetic hero to admire from a distance. Melville seems to have been aware that something must happen to Billy to change him from the unconscious Adam into the conscious Christ but, in terms of his fable, he cannot make this explicit and the decisive transition has to take place off-stage in the final interview between Billy and Captain Vere.

CLAGGART

Similar insoluble paradoxes are raised by the demonic, the religious passion in reverse. For the demonic must be moved solely by pride, just as the religious must be moved solely by faith and love. Absolute pride cannot be manifested aesthetically because it tolerates no weakness except itself which thinks of itself as absolute strength.

Absolute pride denies that the six other deadly sins are its children and despises them as weakness, being incapable of seeing that it is the source of all weakness. The Devil, therefore, cannot himself be lustful, gluttonous, avaricious, envious, slothful, or angry, for his pride will not allow him to be anything less than proud. He can only pretend in disguise to be any of these without actually feeling them; he can only "act" them. His acts must appear to be arbitrary and quite motiveless. No accurate aesthetic portrayal, therefore, is possible; Iago has to be given some motive, yet if the motive is convincing, he ceases to be demonic.

So with Claggart. Just as the bias in Melville's treatment of Billy Budd is a tendency to identify consciousness and sin, so he makes Claggart identify innocence with love; "To be nothing more than innocent," he sneers on seeing Billy Budd. This is no doubt what the serpent says to Adam, but it is not what he says to himself, which is rather "To be nothing more than loving." For the difference between God and the Devil is not that God does not know the meaning of good and evil and that the Devil does, but that God loves and the Devil will not love. That is why the motive for Claggart's behaviour, half-stated only to be withdrawn because no motive will really do, is homosexual desire.

In *Moby Dick*, where Ahab's pride revolts against lack of absolute strength, against being finite and dependent, the sexual symbolism centres round incest and the Oedipus situation, because incest is the magic act of

145

self-derivation, self-autonomy, with the annihilation of all rival power.

In *Billy Budd*, the opposition is not strength/weakness, but innocence/guilt-consciousness, i.e., Claggart wishes to annihilate the difference either by becoming innocent himself or by acquiring an accomplice in guilt. If this is expressed sexually, the magic act must necessarily be homosexual, for the wish is for identity in innocence or in guilt, and identity demands the same sex.*

Claggart, as the Devil, cannot, of course, admit a sexual desire, for that would be an admission of loneliness which pride cannot admit. Either he must corrupt innocence through an underling or if that is not possible he must annihilate it, which he does.

THE ARTIST AS DON QUIXOTE

To understand the romantic identification of sin with consciousness, we must take it together with two other romantic characteristics, the romantic image of the hero as a mariner, an explorer of novelty, and the

---

* It is not an accident that many homosexuals should show a special preference for sailors, for the sailor on shore is symbolically the innocent god from the sea who is not bound by the law of the land and can therefore do anything without guilt. Indeed, in a book like Genet's *Querelle de Brest*, the hero is at once god and devil. He is adored because, though he is a murderer and a police informer and sexually promiscuous in every sense, though, that is, he loves no one but himself, is, in fact, Judas, yet he remains Billy Budd, the beautiful god who feels neither guilt nor remorse, and whose very crimes, therefore, are a proof of his divinity.

romantic contempt for the bourgeois and respectable, the churl who lives by conventional custom and habit. Is not this nostalgia for innocence precisely the characteristic of the man whose dedicated career is the exploration of the hitherto unknown and unconscious, who is by the very nature of his voyage travelling farther and farther away from unconsciousness; and would not the same man despise most those who have started, cannot go back, yet dare not go forward?

In earlier ages it was the business of the artist to record the great acts and thoughts of others. Hector and Achilles are the heroes; Homer records them. Later the hero might be Truth, and the poet's business to set down what has oft been thought but ne'er so well expressed. The contribution of the poet, that is, was his gift for language.

The characteristic of the Romantic period is that the artist, the maker himself, becomes the epic hero, the daring thinker, whose deeds he has to record. Between about 1770 and 1914 the great heroic figures are not men of action but individual geniuses, both artists and, of course, scientists (but they are not our province) with a religious dedication to furthering knowledge, and the kind of knowledge the artist could obtain was chiefly from himself. Characteristically, the subtitle of Wordsworth's epic poem is "The Growth of the Poet's Mind." Faust, Don Juan, Captain Ahab are not really the heroes of their respective books, but the imaginative projections of their creators, i.e., what they do is not

147

really done as a man of action acts for the sake of the act, but in order to know what it feels like to act. Ahab is, so to speak, what it feels like to be Ishmael the recorder. The artist who has thus to be at once the subject of his experiment and the recorder enjoys excitement and suffers terrors hardly known before. He ceases to have an identity and becomes like the Baker, who cannot remember his name and no longer bakes but hunts. He used to bake bridecake, i.e., his recording of glorious deeds and thoughts strengthened the bonds of community. Now he is a nomad explorer, whose one virtue is his courage that can

> "joke with hyaenas returning their stare
> With an impudent wag of the head."

Further, to become so dedicated to a lonely task, done not for the public but for the sake of the truth, mere talent is insufficient. The romantic artist is a *poète maudit*, i.e., an individual marked out by some catastrophe like Ahab's which supplies the driving passion to go ever forward, to the limits of exhaustion.

Nothing was not to be known, nothing: hysteria, debauchery, disorder, grief, nor despair.

What Rimbaud said of himself in *Une Saison en Enfer* before bidding good-bye to art is true, more or less, one way or another, of them all.

Je m'habituai à l'hallucination simplex: je voyais très franchement une mosquée à la place d'une usine, une école de

tambours faite par les anges, des calèches sur les routes du ciel,
un salon au fond d'un lac; les monstres, les mystères; un titre
de vaudeville dressait des épouvantes devant moi. Puis j'ex-
pliquai mes sophismes magiques avec l'hallucination des mots!

Je finis par trouver sacré le desordre de mon esprit. J'étais
oisif, en proie à une lourde fièvre: j'enviais la félicité des bêtes,
—les chenilles, qui représentent l'innocence des limbes, les
taupes, le sommeil de la virginité.

(Une Saison en Enfer)

Small wonder then if their capacity for experience was
burned out quite early, like Wordsworth's, or if the
ability to express vanished in a welter of feelings, like
Coleridge's, or if the man himself suffered from spleen,
like Baudelaire. More remarkable is the realisation by
some of them that the artist is not, as he had thought,
Don Quixote, the Religious Hero, but only Ishmael, the
explorer of possibility, for whom the Button-Moulder
and the Boojum are waiting at the next cross-roads
where they will be asked to prove whether or no they
have become their actual selves.

Thus Melville:

Round the world! There is much in that sound to inspire
proud feelings; but whereto does all that circumnavigation
lead? Only through numberless perils to the very point whence
we started, where those that we left behind secure were all
the time before us.

Thus Rimbaud:

"I! I who called myself magus or angel, dispensed with all
morality, I am cast back to the soil, with a duty to seek, and

149

enough actuality to grasp! Peasant!—I will ask pardon for
having nourished myself on lies. And now, let us go."

(*Une Saison en Enfer*)

We live in a new age in which the artist neither can
have such a unique heroic importance nor believes in the
Art-God enough to desire it, an age, for instance, when
the necessity of dogma is once more recognised, not as
the contradiction of reason and feeling but as their
ground and foundation, in which the heroic image is
not the nomad wanderer through the desert or over the
ocean, but the less exciting figure of the builder, who
renews the ruined walls of the city. Our temptations are
not theirs. We are less likely to be tempted by solitude
into Promethean pride: we are far more likely to become
cowards in the face of the tyrant who would compel us
to lie in the service of the False City. It is not madness
we need to flee but prostitution. Let us, reading the
logs of their fatal but heroic voyages, remember their
courage.

Melville once wrote a Requiem for soldiers lost in
ocean transports, which seems to me no less fitting a
requiem for him and his brethren in France, England
and America.

All creatures joying in the morn,
Save them forever from joyance torn,
    Whose bark was lost where now the dolphins play;
Save them that by the fabled shore,
    Down the pale stream are washed away,

Far to the reef of bones are borne;
    And never revisits them the light,
Nor sight of long-sought land and pilot more;
    Nor heed they now the lone bird's flight
Round the lone spar where mid-sea surges pour.

WYSTAN HUGH AUDEN was born in York, England, in 1907. He
has been a resident of the United States since 1939, and an
American citizen since 1946. Educated at Gresham's
School, Holt, and at Christ Church, Oxford, he became
associated with a small group of young writers in London—
among them Stephen Spender and Christopher Isherwood
—who became recognized as the most promising of the
new generation in English letters. He collaborated with
Isherwood on several plays; among them are *The Dog
Beneath the Skin* and *The Ascent of F-6* (available as *Two
Great Plays* in Vintage Books).

Mr. Auden is the author of several volumes of poetry,
including *About the House*, *Homage to Clio*, *The Double
Man*, *For the Time Being*, *The Age of Anxiety*, *Nones*, and
The Shield of Achilles, which received the National Book
Award in 1956. His *Selected Poetry* appears in The Modern
Library. A volume of essays, *The Dyer's Hand*, appeared in
1962. *Collected Shorter Poems* and *The Orators* were pub-
lished in 1967.